LABOR'S
RELATION TO CHURCH
AND COMMUNITY

LABOR'S
RELATION TO CHURCH
AND COMMUNITY

A series of addresses

EDITED BY

Liston Pope

Essay Index Reprint Series

Originally published by
THE INSTITUTE for RELIGIOUS and SOCIAL STUDIES

BOOKS FOR LIBRARIES PRESS
FREEPORT, NEW YORK

Library of Congress Cataloging in Publication Data

Institute for Religious and Social Studies, Jewish
    Theological Seminary of America.
    Labor's relation to church and community.

    (Essay index reprint series)
    Original ed. issued in Religion and civilization
series.
    "The chapters of this book grew out of lectures
given...at the institute...in 1944, 1945, and 1946."
    1. Labor and laboring classes--U. S.--1914-
--Addresses, essays, lectures. 2. Church and labor
--U. S.--Addresses, essays, lectures. I. Pope, Liston,
ed. II. Title. III. Series: Religion and civilization series.
HD8072.I5 1972   331'.0973   78-167368
ISBN 0-8369-2657-9

PRINTED IN THE UNITED STATES OF AMERICA
BY
NEW WORLD BOOK MANUFACTURING CO., INC.
HALLANDALE, FLORIDA 33009

TO THE

MEMORY AND CONTINUING INFLUENCE OF

Louis D. Brandeis

Walter Rauschenbusch

John A. Ryan

*Pioneers in the relation of religion,
labor and community.*

PREFACE

The wave of strikes in American industry and of proposals for labor legislation since the end of the Second World War has directed public attention forcibly to labor's aims and the relation of the unions to other elements of the community. During the industrial peace, relatively speaking, of the war years, when there were few strikes and government agencies largely displaced normal processes of collective bargaining, comparatively little attention was given to the fundamental trends and long-term goals of labor's development. The great strikes that followed the cessation of international hostilities caught the public unprepared to deal understandingly and honestly with the demands presented by labor. Public opinion and public officials tended to react in terms of stereotyped formulae rather than considered, informed judgments.

More recently there has been considerable speculation, by labor leaders as well as others, as to what labor really wants and where it is going. This present volume represents an effort to contribute to the discussion of these questions. Officials in various fields of labor leadership have been asked to describe labor's achievements, policies, and aims, not only with regard to industrial relations but also with reference to the larger community. Several of them have been asked to deal specifically with the values and faiths by which they strive to live and to lead labor—to give, as it were, their own "spiritual autobiographies." If it appears that too many articles are of this type, it should be remembered that much recent discussion has centered on the quality and inner motivations of labor leadership.

No effort has been made to cover systematically all matters with which labor is prominently concerned. Some of its more salient aims have been chosen for special attention; for comprehensive coverage, one would need to go to the basic books on the American labor movement.

The chapters of this book grew out of lectures given by the various contributors at the Institute for Religious and Social Studies in New York City in 1944, 1945, and 1946. A number of these chapters were first prepared, therefore, while the special conditions of wartime still prevailed, or while the postwar strikes were actually in progress. While all the material has been revised for publication, references to particular situations have been allowed to remain when they help to illuminate some aspect of labor's long-range problems and possibilities.

Miss Jessica Feingold and Mr. George Lindbeck have helped immensely with preparation of the manuscripts for publication.

L. P.

New Haven, Connecticut
August 10, 1946

TABLE OF CONTENTS

I. LABOR AND THE COMMUNITY

I

MEANINGFUL JOBS FOR WHOLE PEOPLE

T. NORTH WHITEHEAD

Harvard University, Graduate School of Business Administration

In our modern industrial civilization it seems inevitable that most people should be paid workers, and it is of the very first importance that their jobs should be meaningful to them. But I suggest that we shall not get much farther in our thinking if we fix our eyes too narrowly on the job, because what has to be made meaningful is not just the job by itself, but the lives of the workers, both when they are on their job and at all other times.

To be meaningful, a man must see his life as an integrated whole in which all his activities bear a relationship to one another. The whole man goes to work. The worker is not an abstraction, an "economic man," but a whole man with his hopes and fears, his customs and his ideals: it is the same man who is at work and at play and in our thinking we must avoid building an artificial barrier between the different parts of the worker's life. It is sometimes difficult to think of the worker's life as a whole, for so much of our theory teaches us to do just the opposite. For instance, the classical economic theory leads us to think of work as a burden to be borne merely for the sake of the recompense. In this view, work is a hardship rather like a visit to the dentist, to be endured for the sake of the well-being that is to follow. Another implication which runs through so much of the classical economic theory is that a man in his working mood and in his working time is pursuing his own personal, or at most his family's, material interest to the complete exclusion of all other purposes. He is supposed to entertain no ideals, sentiments, or desires which conflict with his economic well-being. Finally it seems to be implied that a worker on the job has no human need to associate with other men and does so only to the extent that it will increase the efficiency of his work.

Of course no economist ever believed these implications; nevertheless, economic theory on occasion does seem to rest on assumptions of this kind and we sometimes talk and think in the same way. We divide our worker into two distinct personalities which seem to be unrelated to one another. At work he is an economic, logical machine, while after hours we think of him as an emotional social creature.

According to this view, there are two men inside one skin who seem to have very little connection with one another. Professor Elton Mayo refers to the classical economic theory as the "rabble hypothesis," the hypothesis of human beings milling around without any particular need for one another, with no social structure to bind them together and no human loyalties, associating just in so far as it may promote their individual economic purposes.

Of course, this way of looking at workers entirely ignores men's insistent needs for human association and for the elaboration of social structures which have arisen out of these needs. It ignores our whole social and idealistic nature. Consequently, it ignores, or very seriously minimizes, all those human organizations which have developed to meet our social needs.

Unfortunately, the "rabble hypothesis" is not only used in economic theory; it is to be found almost as much in current political thinking, and it shows itself in many present-day plans for making a better world. Many political plans recognize at one end of the scale single unrelated individuals whilst at the other end stands the nation, the political structure of the great society. But there seems to be almost nothing in between these two extremes in the minds of many political thinkers.

Many of our difficulties come from ignoring the whole richness and variety of life in its human relationships. This applies to our political thinking, and it applies just as much when we are considering the human problems of industry. We tend to ignore the great variety of human associations which are necessary to the well-being of every worker from the janitor to the president.

When we think of a man at his work, what should we be thinking about? Work is not merely a preparation for living; it is the very act of living. Moreover, broadly speaking, a very large proportion of all the things we do in life is in some sense of the word economic; that is to say, they are a preparation for the future. Most of our life is a preparation for our future; that is what living consists of. When we make our beds in the morning we are preparing for the future, not the very distant future perhaps, but nonetheless we are preparing for the future. When we eat a meal, that also is a preparation for the future. That same activity is not only a preparation for the future, it is also a source of satisfaction in the present. Almost all acts which are important to us are at one and the same time a source of present satisfactions and a preparation for the future. Moreover, most important acts, such as eating a meal, are essentially social in their nature; we do them together with other people and we have elaborated codes of behavior and a whole set of customary ways which both make for efficiency and enhance our personal satisfactions. A certain part of this process of living has become highly organized in relatively modern times. This highly organized segment of our lives we refer to as our business or as our job, and it is that part of life, and that part only, which we commonly think of when we talk of the worker at his work. From a technical point of view, our paid jobs probably represent the most efficient of all our activities, but it also seems true that it is our paid jobs which are most apt to fail in human satisfactions.

Why should that be? Let us approach this by asking ourselves another question: let us think of any of our acquaintances who seem to us to be leading thoroughly useful lives which are satisfying both to themselves and to those around them. What is characteristic of such people? To me the most outstanding characteristic of such people is that their lives are importantly guided by their sense of obligation or loyalty to the individuals and groups which go to make up their world. Like all of us, such people belong to quite a number of different groups, but they differ from others in the degree to which they have identified their own satisfactions with the well-being of their various groups.

Successful, stable groups enable their members to experience social satisfactions in the present while working for their future. These two elements of a worthwhile life are inseparable in any healthy activity. Living merely for the pleasures of the moment becomes a bore in the long run and, equally, the present cannot always be sacrificed for the future. The dentist's chair is an obvious example of sacrificing the present for the future, and no one could stand much of that.

These groups to which we belong are of very different kinds both in their satisfactions and their purposes. A factory has a clearly defined purpose, while the members of a family perhaps do not think of the family as having a purpose at all, although clearly it has many purposes and many satisfactions. In varying degrees we find purposes and satisfactions in a group of intimate friends, in clubs and societies, in churches, in community affiliations, and in political groups of all sorts. It is surely satisfying to the citizens of this country that they should be developing good-neighbor relations with the republics of Latin America—this is a very large group, but it yields purposes and satisfactions for many of the individuals comprising it.

Satisfactory living seems to involve a wide variety and complication of human relationships and organizations which give scope for the various facets of human interest. At the same time this complexity must make sense to those experiencing it, otherwise their lives become chaotic. No one can stand chaos for long. To make sense, a man's life must make a single whole to him, in which the parts fit together without too much strain. When a situation looks chaotic, then no fairly simple line of conduct or system of ethics or of interests suffices to cover the whole situation, and the individual becomes bewildered and dissatisfied. It is in achieving this unity of living in the midst of complication that I think most serious moral problems arise. I suggest that most of our moral problems are not to be expressed in the time-honored form of sin *versus* virtue; that is far too simple a concept. Our real moral problem is that of building a meaningful unity out of the possibilities and alternatives around us. This is the problem of organizing our technical and moral aspirations into a compatible way of life; it involves both our intellectual and our emotional natures.[1]

With this in mind, let us return to the problem of "how to make jobs meaningful" or, rather, how to make the worker's life meaningful to him when he is on the job. We must admit, on the evidence, that only too often his working life is profoundly unsatisfying.

Industry and business generally do not suffer from a lack of purpose or from inefficiency in their technical processes as compared with the rest of life. What is more, business is not lacking in a well-developed level of morality as compared with human behavior in general. People who know little about it are apt to regard business as a rather dirty "skin-game," but this is not the view of those who know most about the business world. Many people who pride themselves on a high level of professional conduct do not in practice show any superiority to business in this respect.

But while business is well organized and well led to achieve its technical purpose—to care for the future—it is not usually so well arranged to give its workers the satisfactions of human relationship in the present. It is not so many years ago that we used to hear the expression "business is business." This was used to mean that only technical, including economic, considerations were relevant to business leadership. This was a plea for the adoption of the rabble hypothesis, in which the social instincts of man were to be neglected during working hours. One of the most important changes in business leadership during recent years has been the growing attention to the problem of human satisfactions in working cooperation.

Let us, for a moment, compare an army with a business organization. In any well led army one finds an organization in which great

---

[1] Mr. Chester Barnard has an excellent discussion of executive responsibility in this connection in Part IV of his book, *The Functions of the Executive*, especially in Chapter XVII.

emphasis is placed on human associations and social loyalties, arranged in a hierarchy of groups all the way from a section or platoon up to an army corps. In every group we find stable human relations built on a pride of comradeship and of cooperative achievement. Loyalty and mutual trust are the foundation stones of army morale and their absence is the fundamental military sin. This corporate morale enables a soldier to go through the most extraordinary hardships and dangers, unknown to the average civilian, and often to come through with his morale unshaken. Of course, an army type of organization is far too simple a pattern for civilian life. The purpose of an army is a simple one and it does not have to cater to the complexities of a full social existence. Nevertheless, the morale of an army gives a clue to many civilian problems. It points out the importance of stable groups built on comradeship, loyalty and mutual obligation in the service of a purpose, or purposes, with a leadership devoted to these ends.

Superficially, any large business is organized somewhat on army lines. You find a factory divided into large sections, each with its separate shops, and smaller working groups within each shop. Every level has its appointed "commander," all the way from the plant manager through the foreman to the junior supervisor. But, on a closer view, it will be found that relatively little attention is given to building up group fellowships and their attendant loyalties. The leaders are all immersed in the technical and organizational problems that confront them. As compared with a modern business, an army has traditionally been a relatively unprogressive organization, though this may have been less often true recently. In many industries continued change is forced by the pressure of technological discovery. This creates a real difficulty for business leadership. Business executives have the task of building up and maintaining group loyalties without so "freezing" the situation as to hamper the organization in its competitive struggle or to produce a dreary absence of development. For people need the sense of movement, provided this does not result in a total lack of stable associations. The problem is to achieve a flexible organization with a sufficiency of social stability. This is not an impossibility, but it calls for a very high type of leadership and, above all, for leaders who understand the full scope of their problem. The days when technical skill sufficed for leadership in business have gone by, if, indeed, they ever really existed. The great attention which is now being paid to the training of foremen is evidence of a change for the better in this respect.

But the problem cuts deeper still, for stable groups are essential to human satisfaction whether in the factory or elsewhere. But every group builds up its own pattern of thought, behavior, and customs, as it should, and the real problem of leadership is to help these groups to work together in amity without destroying each other's individual characters. A group without its individual character would be a contradiction in terms, but it is all too easy for a group to develop an intolerance for any character besides its own and so defeat its possibility of working with others to build up a larger organization. Cooperation between groups is one of the biggest problems of leadership whether in business, or politics, or international affairs. It is no answer to try to suppress group loyalties, for they give the satisfactions of living. Where suppression is attempted, as it often is in business, the result is a poor life with little satisfaction, or the emergence of rebel groups which develop in opposition to the organizations of which they are a part. We have all encountered rebel groups, and when we get to know them we find their life is not very satisfying to them: they are all a little sour. We all want our groups to expand and lead toward some larger and wider purpose, but this involves associating with others in a spirit of good will and reasonable security.

So, to make the worker's life meaningful, what is needed is a leadership which pays equal attention to both the social and the technical needs of its people. I am not suggesting a return to an outworn form of paternalism. A paternalistic leader is one who forces on others his idea of what is good for them, instead of studying them to find out what in fact they really desire and then helping them to get it. I want to make this very clear. I am not saying that a management should be soft with its employees any more than it should be tough. Both attitudes are equally unrealistic and sentimental. I am saying that to get the best out of people they must be led in accordance with their real natures, and not in the dim light of some unrealistic generalizations about "economic man." The purpose of business administration is to do business, to stay in business, to make a profit, and go on making a profit, not only today but tomorrow and the day after.

There is nothing wrong with the profit motive; properly understood, it is a high ideal and a law of life. For there can be no such thing as continuing activity without net profit in some important sense. If more effort and energy are being put into work than comes out of it, obviously the work will come to an end for want of something more to put in. If it took more energy to eat than the calorific value of the food taken in, then a meal would end in starvation and death. In a broad sense, human energy must show a profit on the whole if it is to maintain itself. The balance sheet of a firm is a convention which does not tell the whole story, but it is the best technical device known for seeing whether the firm is putting out more than it takes in. People who object to profits are really objecting to some particular form of distribution or ownership; but that is another story. There is nothing wrong with the profit motive; my thesis is that business managements tend to reduce their profits by failing to satisfy the social propensities of their workers. Thus the workers lose the satisfactions of comradeship in a well-run enterprise.

It is all very well to ask that a business administration pay due attention to the peculiarities of the human beings whose cooperation is essential to the enterprise, but this is easier said than done. The world has spent literally billions of dollars in learning how to study steel and other industrial materials. Untold wealth has also been spent in working out the technical methods of organization and control in business. But very little money has gone into the study of human beings in their working lives. I know there are a few psychologists, but I am not thinking about the study of rats in a trap, or the study of people in a laboratory, useful as these may be. I am thinking of the systematic study of men and women in their daily vocations, whether in industry, in church, in politics, or in anything else. Human society is practically an unknown field for research, and it is difficult to see how business and industrial organizations can be run to the satisfaction of their workers until this extreme form of ignorance has been overcome. This achievement depends primarily on the organizations themselves; when they put as much money and enthusiasm into the investigation of their human material as they do into their technical problems, then we shall begin to understand how to reach job satisfaction, and we shall be living in a far more truly profitable world for all concerned.

The simplest and dullest forms of repetitive tasks are precisely those which can most easily be mechanized. These jobs at their worst are the result of a semimechanical age through which we are passing; they will eventually be done by machinery. In this view workers will emerge as people of general skills, capable of supervising a mass of complex machinery rather than as "hands" performing the mechanical actions themselves.

Even a man doing a perfunctory and repetitive task at a machine, without any sight of the end product or of its ultimate uses for society, can come to feel that he is doing an essential piece of work. I have seen exceedingly repetitive jobs performed with obvious enjoyment by whole groups when their human relationships have been well developed with real pride in their cooperative purpose. However interesting our work may be to us, we all find that considered bit by bit most of it is essentially dull. The interest arises out of the larger purpose as developed by our colleagues and our society.

In any case, I believe it to be a mistake to suppose that human beings dislike routine as such; we could none of us live without it. At least as many people are broken by being given responsibilities above their strength as by being used below their capacities. The chief need, I believe, is that in the doing of our work we shall feel ourselves to be contributing responsibly to our immediate society, and this brings us back to the question of an adequate social and technical leadership. This is not a complete answer, for there will be dull jobs for as long as we can see; but I believe that the present disastrous frequency of these jobs could be greatly reduced.

II

LABOR'S CONCERN FOR THE NATIONAL WELFARE

BY

LAWRENCE ROGIN

Educational Director, Textile Workers Union of America

It is the general feeling among Americans that labor has a selfish interest. We hear talks about labor, we read in the newspapers about labor pressures, and one gets the inevitable feeling that those who comment adversely are thinking of the union movement as selfish and interested only in its own concerns. We forget a great deal of American history when we do that.

Not many of us recall how public education in this country developed. A major cause of its development was the concern of labor for education. The trade unions of the 1820's had as one of their aims the establishment of free public education. The right to vote had just been granted to men, without too many property qualifications. The unionists felt that if their children were going to exercise their right to vote intelligently they should have an opportunity for free public education. That early interest in education has characterized the American labor movement for more than one hundred years. We still find in the labor movement a group that has a very great concern with public education, with education of all kinds.

The very right to vote itself, which we now take for granted, was greatly restricted by property qualifications in our early history. Here again the labor movement was concerned with the extension of the franchise, something which today is reflected in the demand by all branches of American labor for the elimination of the poll tax.

But those things do not come to our minds very much when we think about the labor movement. So labor ought to take every opportunity to tell the public of its general plans and how they affect all of America. It is perhaps labor's fault that you do not know more about us. We have been very much concerned with fighting battles, establishing the right to organize, establishing collective bargaining in industries, building our organizations so they can function democratically themselves. We have forgotten that, because we are a large movement that does affect everyone in the country, we have a public relations job to do, a job which is just as important as the one on which the National Association of Manufacturers spends millions of dollars every year. Unfortunately, we do not have that amount of money to spend.

I think it is important for everyone to realize that the general activities that labor carries on are important for the development of democracy within our country. I do not know if any of you traveled into the coal camps of Western Pennsylvania, or into the Southern textile mill villages, prior to the development of unions in those communities. The type of community that existed there was not one in which we would say there was any concern for the welfare of the people. It was mill-dominated, or mine-dominated; the churches, the schools, the newspapers, the street cleaners, the police, were all under the control of the superintendent of the mill, who was sometimes a local person, but more often not, in recent years. There was no education as we think of it. There was no free vote.

I recall that when I lived in Pennsylvania the Secretary of Labor of the United States desired to speak to a meeting of steel workers in Aliquippa. The only place she could speak was from the post office steps, because that alone was a federal building. There was no other hall available. When other persons came there to speak to the workers they had the choice of leaving or being beaten up.

Aliquippa is a different kind of town now, since the steel workers moved in there. The people of Aliquippa began to assert their rights. Now they vote freely, without fear of being fired if they vote contrary to the boss's orders. They have representation in public affairs. It is now what we like to think of as an American community, and not what it was before: a concentration camp in which steel was produced.

The same story could be told about coal camps in West Virginia, Kentucky, Western Pennsylvania, and about hundreds and hundreds of textile towns in North and South Carolina, Virginia, Alabama, and Georgia. The coming of the union has meant that the people of those communities have become citizens of their state, and citizens of the United States. I think that has been a tremendous gain for all of us.

The ordinary job that the union does in getting more money for its members is reflected in these communities, too, in greater prosperity for the middle class, the shopkeepers, the movie theatre owners, and the professional men. When workers do not have enough money to buy food, business people cannot prosper. When there is a spread of the income into working class pocketbooks, then you find greater prosperity in the community.

Collective bargaining likewise contributes a tremendous service to the community and to the nation as well as to labor. The Congress of the United States recognized that when it passed the Wagner Labor Relations Act. I am not so sure all Congressmen who voted for that Act would agree now with their previous judgment, because they have seen unions develop more rapidly than they would like.

But the history of collective bargaining shows that it is a boon to the country because it prevents the kind of industrial strife which has plagued such industries as textiles for half a century. The textile industry never had extensive collective bargaining until about four or five years ago. Yet it is an industry in which there have been probably more and bloodier strikes than in any other industry in the country, not because there were unions, but because there were no unions. Where unions have been established on a firm foundation, as in the garment industries, most of the building trades industries, and the printing industry, machinery is established which permits the settlement of disputes without resorting to strikes.

Some of labor's activities have even a more positive bearing on the welfare of all Americans. First, one could recall some of its contributions to the war effort. We may have now forgotten what was on the tips of our tongues in the latter part of 1940 and early part of 1941, the so-called "Reuther Plan." It was a proposal put forth through the United Auto Workers, CIO, for the immediate conversion of the automobile industry to aid national defense. It was a proposal laughed at by the manufacturers, who said their machinery could not be used for such purposes. Similar proposals were ignored by the steel mill owners, who said there was enough steel if we should need it. But if that proposal had been adopted, it would have meant that we would have been better prepared for defense when the blow fell that threw us into war.

The same spirit which motivated the Reuther Plan and similar union proposals, prevailed in labor circles throughout the war effort. Government officials report that there were more than four thousand so-called labor-management committees which functioned in industrial plants and war production plants in this country under the auspices of the War Production Board. These committees made the greatest contribution toward production where there was an alert and active union in the plant, because the union was concerned about the problems that faced us in getting production.

The figures of war production in this country are astounding. Labor deserves some of the credit for those figures. The estimate by the Secretary of Labor, in discussing the strike statistics for 1944, was that labor had kept the no-strike pledge 99.4 per cent in this country.

The same type of union contribution is evident in the attitude toward such causes as the National War Fund, Red Cross donations, the blood bank, and the purchase of war bonds. There are a lot of statistics about those things; one concrete example may be more illuminating. In Danville, Virginia, there are some fourteen thousand textile workers working for one company. Through 1942, the greatest amount ever raised from those workers in any Community Fund drive was three thousand dollars. There was no union in the plant at that time. When the War Fund Drive took place in 1943, community leaders enlisted the aid of the union. The union undertook the responsibility seriously. The workers went over the top of the goal of twenty-five thousand dollars that was set for them, a rise from three thousand to twenty-five thousand. The workers felt that they owed an obligation to the War Fund, and they felt, too, that they could take the word of their own union representatives that the money would be used wisely for necessary purposes. What happened in Danville, happened all over the country in War Fund campaigns.

Of even greater importance is labor's attitude toward the pressing problems that face all of us, now that the war is over. This is more important because not all of us are as concerned about winning the peace as we were about winning the war. Trade-unionists knew that our first job was to win the war. Who should know better than labor that under all kinds of fascism, the unions have been the first to be destroyed? We were concerned with winning the war, but we are concerned also that sweat and blood shall not have been wasted, and that there shall be a peace that shall be permanent.

We are concerned, first of all, that we shall have a lasting peace; that there shall not be again the same worldwide carnage. Our concern is two-fold: as human beings, we do not like to see blood shed under any conditions; secondly, we know that in a world that is constantly preparing for war there cannot be social benefits for the people. Money spent for tanks, battleships, and guns cannot be spent for hospitals, houses, and schools. We cannot have guns and butter!

We are concerned for these reasons, and we feel that the kind of peace that will be made will therefore have to be a just peace. It will have to be a peace that wins the respect of all the peoples of the world, whether they be in Italy or Germany or France or India or China, or in our own nation. It will have to be a peace without imperialism, because if we are going to have an exploitation of the so-called backward nations, we are going to sow the seeds of another war. If we are going to industrialize India and China and Egypt and Siam on the same basis as other nations have been industrialized hitherto, we are going to sow the seeds of the kind of economic rivalries that lead to fascism and war.

We therefore are very much concerned about recent international developments. We are equally bothered by the continuing development of international cartels. We think that cartels are not agencies of national or international welfare, and we support very strongly the stand that has been taken by our own Department of Justice in attempting to break them up.

Within the country we feel that the same energy, the same forethought, the same determination should be put into planning for full employment in the future as was put into planning for full production for the war. We feel that we can get as good results.

There is a good deal of talk about "a return to free enterprise" in this country. We do not know what that means. Does it mean the kind of economic system which has followed very closely the pattern of the famous Hamilton Report on Manufactures to our first Congress which recommended a subsidy system for business, a practice which has generally been followed since that time? Does it refer to the subsidies to business through the high tariff? Were the tremendous land grants to the railroads an evidence of free enterprise?

If a return to "free enterprise" means a return to the kind of conditions which existed in the textile industry, we know that we are opposed to it. We do not want to return to wages of $6 and $7 a week for fifty hours of work. I myself have seen pay envelopes for girls who went into the mills in the early 1900's, both in the South and in New England. They earned 3 cents an hour, $1.50 a week! Then it was common for a child to be whipped because he was not working fast enough. That was some time ago, but even in the period just prior to the war we had not got away from the malnutrition, poor housing, and the lack of decent schools.

In the textile industry, it is estimated that workers once worked three full months out of twenty-four. Twenty-one months of part time work and unemployment were common. The unions do not want to return to that in the textile or any other industry.

We feel that it is necessary for the government to share in the planning which must prevent such conditions. It is a responsibility of the government to do this. We recognized that it was the responsibility of the government to take a very important share in planning war production. People do not feel that there is anything wrong with that kind of government action; nor is there anything wrong with governmental planning for full employment in peace.

We are concerned, as I said, with getting full employment. That involves a number of different kinds of problems. A pamphlet issued by the CIO Postwar Planning Committee stated the objectives of labor, and I think that this would apply to all labor as well as to the CIO. Labor's peacetime objectives are:

(1) A job at decent wages, or a farm or business that pays; (2) a well built, convenient home, decently furnished; (3) good food, clothing, and medical care; (4) good schooling for children, with an equal chance for healthy and happy growth; (5) an adequate income through social insurance in case of sickness, old age, early death of the wage-earner, or unemployment—not just for the worker, but for all people.

We think there are some concrete things that must be done to accomplish this. One is planning for full employment, with the government playing a part. All of us have been staggered by the statistics on the amount of unemployment we may ultimately have if we do not plan. We must plan in face of the fact that we have never had full employment in this country, that at the time when the war started there were perhaps seven million unemployed, and that the productivity of American labor has gone up tremendously in the past few years.

So we must plan, taking into consideration all elements in our community.

Underlying all of this, there must be a social security program such as was represented by the Wagner-Murray-Dingell Bill, which proposed to extend social security in two ways. The first was by bringing within the scope of the present social security program a large group now excluded: farm and domestic employees, the self-employed, employees of non-profit organizations. It would set up a national system of unemployment compensation to succeed the hodge-podge of systems that now exist. The bill also proposed important first steps toward the establishment of a proper medical care program.

We think there should be some form of health insurance in this country. We are the only democratic government that has not made large strides forward in that field. There will not be adequate medical care for the people in our country until some such system is set up.

We must think also in national terms about many matters which were first thought of as local matters. Medical care is one, social insurance is one, and education is another. The people of South Carolina are spending a higher percentage of their per capita income for education than are the people of New York. For the higher percentage of per capita income, the people of South Carolina get schools that we would not want to send our children to. We cannot provide a decent schooling for the children in Mississippi, North Carolina, and Georgia unless we think in national terms. There must be federal grants to equalize educational opportunity.

Those are our peacetime concerns, and we feel that they are extremely important. We feel that they represent considered thinking by a group of people who have made a contribution toward American life in peacetime and toward winning the war. And we think that around concerns of the kind discussed here, all well-thinking Americans can rally to see that we establish something better in the world than there has been.

III

ORGANIZED LABOR AND CHILDREN

BY

KATHARINE F. LENROOT

Chief, Children's Bureau, U.S. Department of Labor

In Stuart Chase's book, *Democracy Under Pressure*, he quotes from an article by J. Raymond Walsh as follows:

> I believe the greatest single object of organized labor should be graduation from the purely pressure-group approach to problems of hours and wages, prices and working conditions, to one of national leadership in the welfare of this country.[1]

There are 41,550,000 children and youth in this country under the age of eighteen years. They have no vote and no voice in public affairs. The kind of homes in which they live, the health protection they receive, the schools they attend, the patterns of association and behavior they establish, are determined by adults: parents, teachers, friends, voters, contributors to community funds, and those responsible for the professional services which are involved in the nation's greatest and most important undertaking—the rearing of a new generation.

Children cannot form a pressure group. But to people who care, the pressure of their wants and needs is more compelling than any other pressure. To translate concern for individual children into social policies promoting the health, well-being, and opportunity of all children, requires organized effort. The interests of children

---

[1] Quoted from *Antioch Review*, Summer, 1943, in *Democracy Under Pressure, Special Interests vs. the Public Welfare*, Number 4 in the series of guide lines to America's future as reported to the Twentieth Century Fund, New York, 1945, p. 79.

should receive support from all groups in the population organized for purposes which include the molding of public policy. Since children cannot themselves be a pressure group, they should receive support from all pressure groups, for in promoting the welfare of all children regardless of the occupation, economic interests, race, or creed of their parents, we are safeguarding the welfare of the whole nation.

Some 15,000,000 Americans are members of labor organizations, the great majority in the two major bodies—the American Federation of Labor and the Congress of Industrial Organizations. Substantial numbers are enrolled in the Railroad Brotherhoods and other independent organizations. Stuart Chase estimates that about thirty per cent of all workers whose occupations would make them eligible for union membership are now enrolled as members. Organized labor is at its greatest strength in the history of the country. In addition to members of unions, wives of members organized in auxiliaries are beginning to exercise considerable influence.

Labor has consistently served as a pressure group for children, and in the course of years has broadened its interests and outlook to cover many aspects of child life. In many respects, however, labor's concern for children is still expressed in tentative and experimental ways, which will probably be much further developed within the next few years.

National measures in behalf of children, to which organized labor throughout the years has given important—and frequently dominant—support, include the establishment and extension of free schools, the regulation of child labor, the establishment of the Federal Children's Bureau, and the Social Security Act with its important provisions for family security and maternal and child welfare.

During the war period very significant local developments took place under the leadership of the National CIO War Relief Committee and the Labor League for Human Rights (A. F. of L.) working in cooperation with Community Chests and Councils, Inc.

What are some of the major problems affecting children and youth to which the American people must direct their attention, now and in the immediate future?

They have to do with problems of family support: the basic income available to families, the special problems of migrant families, the income available to incomplete or disrupted families—a group greatly augmented by war pressures and war casualties.

They have to do with child labor; during the war the age group 14 to 19 furnished a greater addition to the labor force than any other age group; some 3,000,000 boys and girls 14 to 18 years of age were at work, half of them full time and half on a combined school and work schedule.

They have to do with a chance to attend school and with the kind of education schools provide. In 1940 approximately 2,000,000 children of 6 to 15 years were not attending school.

They have to do with health protection and with medical care in illness. Some forty per cent of all registrants for selective service were found to be physically or mentally unfit for military service.

They have to do with many other aspects of child life: work opportunity for children of suitable age; recreation and leisure-time pursuits; care of children whose mothers are employed; care of children who have lost their parents; juvenile delinquency; getting children out of jail; adoption; child guardianship; illegitimacy; runaway children.

They have to do with assuring equal access to opportunities and services to children of all racial groups.

They have to do above all—and this is a matter of special concern for churches and church leaders—with the basic question for America, the meaning and values attached to life, to personal freedom, to joint effort to achieve common ends, to the disciplines and values inherent in America's heritage and determining America's future.

The children with whom we are concerned are the children of workers, of farmers, of business and professional men, of the self-employed. What do the history of organized labor's concern for children and its present programs hold of promise for the cause of childhood?

That great student of labor history, John R. Commons, lists education as one of the two chief concerns of the first organized labor movements in the United States, becoming active about one hundred and twenty years ago. The voice of labor has been consistently lifted in support of free schools and universal educational opportunity of both a liberal and a vocational character. The American Federation of Labor was chiefly responsible for the passage during the First World War of the first act providing federal aid for vocational education. Organized labor has consistently supported federal aid bills for general elementary and secondary education and has advocated the passage of such a bill before committees of Congress.

In testimony presented on January 30, 1945, before the Senate Committee on Education and Labor, on S-181, Federal Aid to Education, Kermit Eby, Director of the CIO Department of Education and Research, said in part:

Our support of these federal aid to education bills is consistent with labor's historic support of free public education. As early as 1825, when the first political party of workers was set up in Philadelphia, the establishment of free public schools was a prominent plank in the party's platform. . . . And all historians in the field of education agree that it was the workers' organizations which gave continued aid to Horace Mann and other pioneers of public education.

Before the formation of the CIO, our brother labor organization, the American Federation of Labor, consistently tried to secure better schools, properly trained and paid teachers, and federal support to equalize educational opportunity, especially in the interest of the poorer states.

The labor movement led the way to establishing vocational education, and each convention of both the CIO and the A. F. of L. has expressed continued concern through resolutions supporting education.

Free schools are of no avail if child labor robs the child of his chance to attend school. Many thousands of children in families of migrant agricultural laborers, even today, are denied this chance.

The American Federation of Labor since its organization has worked for the prohibition of child labor. As long ago as 1888, the Federation was urging a constitutional amendment to prohibit the employment of children under fourteen in workshops, mines, and factories. In 1917 it demanded still higher standards by adopting the resolution "That the American Federation of Labor is unalterably opposed to the employment of children under sixteen years of age." The Federation has led in the fight for legislation, both federal and state, to prevent the exploitation of child life for private gain. It supported the Palmer-Owen Bill before Congress in 1914, the First Federal Child Labor Law passed in 1916, and the Federal Child Labor Tax Law enacted in 1919. When that law was declared unconstitutional in 1922, the Federation entered the fight for a constitutional amendment placing beyond dispute the power of Congress to act in this field.

It was the president of the American Federation of Labor who headed the Permanent Conference for the Abolition of Child Labor, composed of more than twenty national organizations, which worked for the favorable consideration by Congress of a child labor amendment. When the amendment was submitted to the states in 1924, the Federation began and continued its active work for ratification. Only twenty-eight states have ratified the amendment, eight short of the number needed to make the amendment become part of the Constitution.

The American Federation of Labor also supported the child labor provisions of the Fair Labor Standards Act of 1938.

Not only the A. F. of L. and the CIO but also the Railroad Brotherhoods and other labor organizations have consistently supported measures for the elimination of child labor and for educational opportunity.

Since 1934, the Secretary of Labor has called together annually a "National Conference on Labor Legislation," composed of state labor officials and representatives of organized labor in the states. In 1940 the Conference requested that a small committee be appointed to review the problems of education and training in relation to the welfare of wage earners and their families. In accordance with this request the Committee on Education and Training was appointed, and reported to the eighth conference, in November, 1941. This report was approved unanimously by the Conference.

One of the recommendations of the Committee dealt with the participation of labor in the planning and administration of educational programs.

Organized labor, the Conference recommended, should "be given representation on an equal basis with other elements in the community in the planning of education programs through membership on boards of education, on advisory committees, and on other policy-making bodies." Studies of the composition of local boards of education have shown only very small percentages (some three or four per cent) from the ranks of organized labor.[2]

The resolutions of both the American Federation of Labor and the Congress of Industrial Organizations, adopted in their 1944 conventions, reveal the wide range of labor's support of measures for the better health, education, and well-being of children and youth. The American Federation of Labor, for example, urged a comprehensive program of educational reconstruction which would adapt our educational system to the needs of postwar society. It endorsed the principle of federal aid for elementary and secondary education. The report of the Executive Council on Federal Aid, adopted by the Convention, contained the following statement:

The Nation should thank God for the foresight and perseverance of Samuel Gompers who battled, often against overwhelming opposition, to secure federal aid for vocational and technical education under the Smith-Hughes Act during World War I. Organized labor today is equally emphatic in its demand for federal aid to equalize educational opportunities so that every child in the Nation may be prepared to render the best possible service to his country in peace or in war—whether his place of birth happens to be in the poorest district of the poorest State or in the richest district of the richest State.

The 1944 Convention of the American Federation of Labor made a part of the official proceedings of the 1944 Convention and referred to the permanent committee on education for further study a statement, "In behalf of Youth," submitted by the Children's

[2] "Labor and Education," CIO Publication No. 99, pp. 3–4.

Bureau to President Green. This statement dealt with the principles which should govern public policy with regard to children and youth, and more intensively, with the problems of child labor and youth employment in the reconversion period, and the urgent need for a nationwide program of health protection for mothers and children.

The Congress of Industrial Organizations, in its 1944 convention, adopted resolutions supporting programs for maternal and child health, school lunches, federal aid to education, youth security, and the health and safety of young workers. In its resolution on Maternal and Child Health, the CIO declared "the right of all mothers and children, whatever their race, residence, or family income, to all diagnostic and curative medical services they need for good health." As a first step toward supplying this care now, it was recommended that the CIO "work for an expansion of the maternal and child health and crippled children's programs under the Social Security Act which will make available at public expense whatever medical services are needed to assure the good health of all our mothers and children." The resolution on Youth Security (No. 31), I quote in full:

WHEREAS, (1) Postwar employment, education and security are a major concern of young people as well as of labor, industry, and government, and according to current estimates about five million men and women in the Armed Forces who will be demobilized will be under twenty-two and two million under twenty-one, and

(2) The number of teen age workers in industries and in the Army has expanded by two and one-half millions, and over 500,000 more fourteen to nineteen year old girls are employed in industry now than in normal times —the largest single increase in the nation's total labor force coming from among youth of teen age; and

(3) Special measures must be worked out to (a) absorb into peacetime employment these large numbers of young workers who must work to sustain themselves, (b) withdraw from the immediate labor market a large number of young people by giving them the chance to continue some form of schooling, vocational, or other training. Therefore, be it

RESOLVED, that this CIO convention go on record for (1) A broad government program for training and retraining young workers in new vocations or at higher skills to be put into operation during the reconversion period;

(2) The participation of labor, industry, and government in re-establishing and strengthening all Federal and State laws protecting the work standards governing young workers and young women workers in particular;

(3) A program of Federal and State aid to education, assuring an opportunity for young workers now in industry, who qualify for entry into college, to do so;

(4) The establishment of strict controls over work of minors, and the strict enforcement of existing laws and the enactment of new state legislation to secure the full abolition of child labor below 16 years of age;

(5) The establishment of a permanent National Youth Service Administration that shall serve as a coordinating agency in solution of reconversion and postwar problems of youth.

One of the most significant developments of the war was labor's growing awareness of its responsibility for community planning and the development of community services. This interest in health and welfare programs on the part of the A. F. of L. was represented by the Labor League for Human Rights, which employed a Director of Community Services. The purposes of the League were to inform labor about the services provided by social agencies; to stimulate greater use of these services by labor; to encourage participation of labor in social planning; and to provide for the extension of health and welfare services so that the needs of the community are better served. The League had regional directors and regional offices throughout the United States, which by the fall of 1944 had assisted in the establishment of a hundred and ninety-seven local labor participation committees and eleven state committees.

Established in 1941 for similar purposes, the National CIO War Relief Committee promoted financial support of worthy community welfare and health agencies, labor representation on governing boards and working committees, and interpretation of community services and of workers' needs. The Community Services Division was established in January, 1944, to develop year-round relationships between CIO unions and welfare agencies for the purpose of (a) interpreting existing community services to union members;

(b) interpreting the problems and point of view of workers and their unions to welfare agencies; and (c) developing machinery at the local and national levels through which workers might utilize better existing welfare services and bring about the strengthening and extension of such services in areas where they are inadequate. At a joint conference of representatives of the National CIO War Relief Committee, the Labor League for Human Rights, and Community Chests and Councils, Inc., in September, 1943, a "Joint Suggestion for Labor Participation in Domestic Social Welfare and Health Work" was drafted. This recommended that councils of social agencies establish within their own machinery "Labor Participation Committees," to interpret labor's needs and point of view to councils and their affiliated agencies and planning committees, to interpret the programs and services of the councils and their agencies to unions, and to develop labor leadership for participation on welfare agency boards and committees.

A memorandum entitled "A Partial Listing of Union Activities in the Health and Welfare Fields on Matters Other than Fund Raising," prepared by the National CIO War Relief Committee in September, 1944, listed the activities under the following headings: union counseling, information and referral services; the health field; the recreation field; the child-care and youth field; education for union-social work cooperation; union personnel in agencies on non fund-raising year-round jobs; the housing field; and community services committees and labor participation committees. An example of the first type of activity, union counseling, information and referral services, is the Camden, New Jersey, Union Organization of Social Services, originally centered about referral work and guidance for juvenile delinquents. The organization was admitted to the Community Chest. CIO committees have joined with other community groups to establish teen age recreation centers. In a number of cities CIO unions have set up child care committees, or have joined with other groups in working on problems of child care of children whose mothers are employed. Some unions have surveyed the need for nursery and day care centers and have publicized facilities available to union members. In a few places unions run their own child care centers. The labor press has carried a great many articles on the child care situation. Unions have also worked with social agencies to make summer camping available to the children of their members.

Locally, responsibility for these activities under the CIO is sponsored by two kinds of community committees. The first is a CIO Community Services Committee appointed by the local Industrial Union Council, to serve as a coordinating body for activities of all CIO unions in the health and welfare field. In September, 1944, such committees existed in some sixty cities. Secondly, labor participation committees in councils of social agencies, usually having equal representation from CIO, A. F. of L., and the social work field, were in existence in some thirty cities.

In a few cities, as Detroit, Cleveland, and Columbus, councils of social agencies have had special liaison staff members to work with the labor liaison staff and the unions.

In a statement made to the welfare committee of the Offices of Community War Services, Federal Security Agency, the Director of the CIO Community Services Division said:

On the whole, the policy of the War Relief Committee is to discourage the institution of union-sponsored welfare services where they may duplicate existing effective or potentially effective community-wide services. Labor for many years has been isolated from the community and the community from labor. The committee is interested not only in building better unions, but better communities.

The aims of organized labor for children and youth, with respect to both national and local policies and programs, are in general the same as the aims of the churches. Prominent among the social action programs of both Christian and Jewish religious bodies have been support of educational opportunity; elimination of child labor; the establishment of the Federal Children's Bureau; opportunities for children of migrant families; opportunities for all children whatever their race, creed, or national origin. The Church, which serves all people regardless of economic or occupational interests, has very special responsibilities for the building of communities where children and youth may be assured the safeguards and the opportunities which are essential to their health and growth. Church people have a vital stake in community planning and in the policies and administration of health, educational, social, welfare and other community services, as well as in the programs of the federal government and of the states in furthering security and opportunity for all.

In considering some of the major issues which will be before the people of this country in the years to come, the question of the basic values which underlie individual action and social policy is especially the concern of religion, which by definition should be an influence binding together diverse interests and points of view. The problem of choice between two goods is always more baffling than the choice between good and evil. Many a mother has to choose between devoting her time to her home and children, and gainful employment which may bring the family income up to a level where the basic family needs may be decently met, but may be costly in terms of the nurture and supervision of her children. It is easy to see that when mothers, for national interest or family support, have to work, the community has a responsibility to make good care available to their children. Probably we would all agree that in a free country a mother has a right to make up her own mind, in consultation with the father and other members of the family, as to whether she will seek gainful employment. At the same time that we hold to the principles of freedom of choice we must see that the choice really is free; that social policy as expressed through such programs as social security, aid to dependent children, and community services, places as much value upon the mother's devotion of her time and strength to the care of children as it places upon wage earning. We must see that child care services do not become a substitute for economic policies that make it possible for a father to earn a reasonable livelihood for his family without the mother's needing to be employed, or for provision of substitutes for the father's earnings when death, disability or other cause removes them as an element in family support.

Consideration of these problems, which involve not only the

time which a mother can devote to her children, but also the time allowed by fathers for companionship with their sons and daughters, should be a responsibility of both church and labor groups, as well as of public officials and private agencies responsible for community services.

Comparable problems face young people as they reach working age. We are becoming increasingly convinced of the importance of postponing entrance into full-time employment until an education fully suited to the youth's capacities has been obtained. But we are still uncertain as to the ways in which society may have to supplement family earnings, if education is to be really available to all promising youth.

The tasks ahead of labor in this country with reference to children relate to the extension of public services so that children everywhere may be assured access to all those services and facilities that are necessary for their health, education, growth, and development. In setting our objectives for children we must not forget the basic problem of an adequate level for family support—an objective directly within the field of organized labor. It must not be thought that our goals for children can be achieved through action by the federal government alone. The development within recent years of the A. F. of L. and CIO organizations for encouraging the participation of labor in community planning and community services, is a most promising sign of the recognition by labor of responsibility for community as well as national action. More than any unit of government, the state is entrusted with basic responsibilities for the protection of children and the provision of opportunities for their health, education, and advancement. It is to be hoped that similar effective relationships can be developed between state bodies representing organized labor, departments of state government and statewide agencies, as those which have already been achieved in many communities through labor participation committees. Support of state legislation as well as improvement in state services is a matter of urgent importance. One of the measures now pending in a number of states is that of raising to sixteen years the minimum age of admission to gainful employment under state law during hours when school is in session, and for employment at any time in manufacturing occupations.

Above all, we must have in this country on the part of all groups the concern for the welfare of all the people which has been expressed in some of the statements of organized labor with reference to children and youth which I have cited. As children have led us in the past to more decent and humane policies for all age groups, so they should lead us to the daily practice of our conviction that none of us can know security and freedom unless both security and freedom are available to all.

IV

ORGANIZED LABOR AND EDUCATION [1]

BY

MARK STARR

Educational Director, International Ladies' Garment Workers'
Union

Organized labor and education have been old acquaintances in the past and are close companions now and for the future. The cooperation given by organized labor to the public school system in the past stands clear in the record. Both educators and members of organized labor recognize the great assistance which both groups can give each other in the future.

Every adequate history of education shows that in the early days, when public education was in its promotional stage, Horace Mann and other pioneers received more help from the labor groups than from any other section of the community. According to *History of Labor in the United States* (Vol. I, pp. 169–170, 224), edited and in part written by the eminent labor historian, John R. Commons:

The first awakening of American wage earners as a class did not occur until the late twenties (1820). . . . The cause of the awakening was economic and political inequalities between citizens of different classes, not primarily between employers and wage earners but between producers and consumers. Around two chief grievances, both closely related to their status as citizens of a democracy, the working men of this period rallied. First was the demand for leisure which furnished the keynote of economic movement. . . . Second was the demand for the consideration of public

[1] This lecture was given at the Institute, February 20, 1945. Mr. Starr subsequently used much of the material for the Inglis Lecture, which was published in *Labor Looks at Education*, Harvard University Press.—Ed.

education which furnished the keynote of the political movement. Charity schools were held to be incompatible with citizenship, for they degraded the workmen and failed to furnish them with the requisite training and information for consideration of public questions, thereby dooming them to become dupes of political demagogues. . . . In 1829, public education took its place distinctly and definitely as the head of the list of measures urged by the Working Men's Party. . . . And the candidates for the State Legislature (Pennsylvania) nominated by the Working Men's Party were pledged to favor a general system of state education.

From the Working Men's Party in Philadelphia in 1829 right down to the most recent Conventions of the A. F. of L. and CIO, organized labor has never forgotten the importance of education. Recently, the CIO has issued an attractive pamphlet, "Labor and Education," in which it reiterates the case for better schools and textbooks and adequate pay for teachers. The A. F. of L., the Railroad Brotherhoods, and the CIO have attacked inequalities in education and advocated federal support by which they can be destroyed. It is well to remember that organized labor, now fourteen million strong, is one of the greatest forces fighting to get equality of educational opportunity; no group of organized teachers should overlook this powerful ally. And when we read that 200,000 teachers have quit school in the past three years to get better jobs, the situation demands prompt attention and aid.

While organized labor has done well by the schools, the record of the service of the schools to labor does not show so bright a picture. There are big improvements to be noted in current trends, but much remains to be done to give labor the recognition that it deserves in social studies. The labor unions have, in part, been at fault because they have not endeavored to provide the schools and the textbook writers with the wealth of attractive material lavishly supplied by the National Association of Manufacturers and similar groups.[2]

[2] A letter dated January 19, 1945, from the National Industrial Information Committee of the National Association of Manufacturers, 14 West 49th Street, New York City, and signed by Edgar J. Sherman, Director, Group Relations Department, said in part:

Any discussion of education must involve a consideration of its aim. Perhaps the most noncontroversial definition would be that education should prepare us for life, which, while including a livelihood, is really something greater. Dr. Eduard C. Lindeman, at the Times Hall on January 9, 1945, made the following definition of desired qualities:

Education should be realistic, experimental, and progressive: *Realistic* in the sense that it deals with problems appropriate to the student's interest and experience; *experimental* in the sense that both its means and its ends must be altered in response to new scientific knowledge regarding human nature and society; *progressive* in the sense that it is considered to be man's chief instrument for improvement.

The happiness of a nation does not depend exclusively upon the extent of its world trade or its production statistics. Surely we should agree with John Ruskin that, "There is no wealth but life —life with all its opportunities for joy, admiration, and knowledge. That nation is the richest which has the greatest number of healthy, happy human beings."

Education thus has a negative and a positive job to do. It should inform the individual about the dangerous poison of racial hate just as it warns youngsters about drinking from bottles labeled "Poison." As modern society becomes more complex, there is a greater danger that uninformed, uneducated individuals will throw dangerous boomerangs. The work of the teacher, particularly in the social studies, is indispensable in showing us how social life began and changed through the years. But teachers cannot substitute knowledge about the past for action in the present. They must give the individual information so that he can do something about the social problems of today. Such problems face him, not as

---

"Teachers looking for a new approach to the study of the social sciences have found the *You and Industry* booklets described in the enclosed pamphlet an effective means of stimulating interest in economic, social and civic subjects. More than five million copies of this series of booklets have been requested by teachers of both junior and senior high schools during the past three years."

A prepaid order blank was enclosed for films and pamphlets supplied free upon request.

an individual, but as a unit in an economic group and member of his community. These problems grow more difficult because today the world has become interdependent. We talk too glibly about global war without realizing what that means in expanding our mental horizons. Technical development in transport and communication—for which the tempo of application was intensified stupendously by the needs of wartime—has hardly penetrated our minds. We have not adjusted our ways of thinking and our ways of life to face these changes with safety and satisfaction.

Educators have been handicapped in teaching all they knew because any realistic approach to society stirs up controversy, and the teachers' search for truth is often vigorously resented by people who do not appreciate adverse publicity for the particular vested interest which they cherish. How can the teacher create the necessary social competency and give to the citizen of the future a sense of responsibility in our complex modern age? And also inspire the students to *use* that competency to shape the world of tomorrow?

Suggestions made here must perforce be general, and educators, as the experts and technicians, will have the job of translating these suggestions to suit the relative ages and teaching situations. There can be little doubt that human beings are not born with that respect for the rights of others which is the kernel of the democratic ideal. The school and all of us in the past took democratic rights for granted as we take fresh air and health until we are menaced by their loss. Repetition of the facts of social history or encyclopedic memorizing of dates are no substitute for an understanding of social change. Calendars and almanacs are easily available. Classrooms should not be cages for parrots. Students may be good even if they have neither the trunk nor the alleged retentive powers of the elephant. Progress cannot be built upon a blind idolatry of the past. The real patriots in the United States will acknowledge with shame the existence of Jim Crow and other racial discriminations. They will not endeavor to cover up that one third of a nation which does not have a chance for a decent education. Then, too, the democratic ideal does not repose on velvet in a glass case. It has to be exposed to the hurly-burly of everyday life. It has to be translated into the problems of group living.

All this will compel the intelligent teacher to study the ways of democracy as they influence not only the individual but trade unions, cooperatives, chambers of commerce, manufacturers' associations, and other functioning groups. At various levels, the textbooks in history are doing a much better job than hitherto in recognizing the existence of the labor unions. Among recent textbooks, for example, is *The American Way of Life,* by Faulkner, Kepner, and Pratt (Harper, 1941), which gives good and attractive illustrations of union activity. The textbook, *America's Economic Growth,* by F. A. Shannon, is also at pains to describe the activity of the labor unions. Those interested will also find some good material in *American Democracy—Today and Tomorrow,* by O. and R. Goslin. In 1944, Harper published *Labor in America,* by Faulkner and Starr, the first high school textbook in this field. This, we hope, will fill a gap so far as the fourth year of high school is concerned. Older students will find *The American Story of Industrial and Labor Relations,* published by the New York State Joint Legislative Committee, a useful text. The National Education Association investigation and report, *Learning the Ways of Democracy,* is also helpful and suggestive in this field. This book was published in 1940 by the Educational Policies Commission of the NEA and the American Association of School Administrators. After describing some hopeful experiments, the NEA investigators reported that, apart from rare examples, economic instruction tends often to deal only with remote institutions and affairs. Writing later in *School Life,* December, 1941, Commissioner John W. Studebaker asserted:

Of the 7½ million youth enrolled in our high schools only about 5 per cent receive any systematic instruction in economics. . . . The schools and colleges must do a much better job of teaching economics. . . .

The NEA investigators also noted that modern problems are "usually discussed and studied in isolation," and they make the general comment:

Courses in economics are taught more and more commonly in the American secondary schools, but they are still, for the most part, elective.

Even in most of the schools, only a relatively small number of students enroll in economics classes. As long as economics and modern problems remain elective, it will, unfortunately, be possible for the majority of students to graduate from high school without any systematic instruction in the economic foundations of American life. Study of the economic aspects of our civilization should be required no less than study of the political and cultural.

Most of us in the labor movement feel that the teacher cannot give a fair and adequate picture of social life in the United States if he does not show the great contribution made by labor to community welfare. Labor urges a better teaching about how men and women have solved their bread-and-butter problems in the past and an examination of how social life can be improved in the present and future.

Because labor has failed to secure from the public school system the information and help desired, it has in some instances set up its own educational activities. Those active in the field of workers' education will testify that part of their job is to find an antidote for what has passed as education in many of our school systems. As children, we are given a biased view of history. The warrior who burned the wheat fields is given greater prominence than the reaper who labored therein and the baker who baked the wheat into bread. The captain who destroys a city is hymned, but the stonemason who built the city is one of the forgotten men. Our children are not taught the debt they owe to the unknown heroes who invented the first wheel and the needle and discovered fire.

The imposing rounded periods of the Declaration of Independence and of the Constitution are rightly known to students, but even in Massachusetts the school children have not been told about Daniel Shays and his fellow rebels who had been cheated out of their lands for which they had fought against the British tyrants. You will recall Archibald MacLeish's lines in "Land of the Free":

> Dan Shays is a hole in the Pelham hills:
> His memory is a door stone in the pine trees:
> Boston taught him:
> > Boston embalmer of history
> Blots his name out on the schoolbook page.

The Negro boys and girls in school are rarely if ever told about Nat Turner. Our children are indeed told about Barbara Fritchie ("Shoot if you must this old gray head," etc.) but never about the dauntless courage of Mother Jones as she faced the thugs and the soldiers in the armed camps of the mining towns. Millions of children, sons and daughters of workers, do not even know her name, despite her heroism which, like that of other rebels in those company towns, was equal to that displayed at Valley Forge. It is only in their own union classes that garment workers, for example, learn about the awful tragedy of the Triangle Fire, New York City (March 25, 1911), and the courage and daring of Clara Lemlich and her fellow waistmakers in 1909.

Scant mention, if any, is given in the history books to trade unions and to men like Samuel Gompers and Eugene V. Debs. It is easier to shout "Remember the Alamo" and "Remember Pearl Harbor" than to build the future decently. Very few history books quote the speeches of Abraham Lincoln on the right to strike, on the superior claims of the man above the dollar, on Lincoln's dark foreboding of the coming of the trusts and the domination of big business. Peter Zenger's fight for a free press also receives little attention in the schools. We have forgotten Horace Mann's hope, when he was fighting with labor's aid for free education, that thereby the "servility of Labor" and the "dominance of Capital" would be overcome. Professional patrioteering groups have tried to falsify history to fortify reaction; they have indulged in foolish idolatry of a drum-and-trumpet history.

Some superficial minds will say education must teach facts only and avoid controversial subjects. Yet no real study of facts can be made by isolating facts and making one's mind a depository of disconnected bits and pieces. It is the function of the human mind to organize facts into a comprehensive general pattern and thus interpret them. Willy-nilly we do this, even if unconsciously and badly. Education cannot be mere vaporings of sweetness and light.

A natural desire to soft-pedal antagonisms, plus the mental obsolescence that comes with old age and hardened arteries in men and institutions, should not make us forget that there are specific conflicts in education as elsewhere. In our teaching of civics we cannot maintain full national sovereignty and simultaneously create world citizenship. Scientific thought cannot advance without stirring up the furies of obscurantism. We cannot tell the truth about human beings and nations without provoking the exponents of racism or discuss comparative religion without stirring up a hornet's nest of fundamentalists.

Too often we are lulled into lethargy by the saccharine voices of our radio announcers who in the same breath proclaim the death agonies of a people and the alleged virtues of a laxative. As Morse said, "What hath God wrought!" Education should stop foolishly trying to ignore the facts of individual and social life. Even in New York City reactionary forces prevent competent trained teachers from explaining even to our high school and college students the functions of their bodies, and so young and old suffer. At worst, bobby-sox girls became wartime "pickup girls" and desperate delinquents to be found in our city courts and hospitals. Less seriously, such books as *Forever Amber* are circulated in a million copies.

Perhaps a few words in explanation of what trade unions do directly to remedy the defects of current education will be in place here. Workers' education may be defined as the study of the social sciences and related courses for the purpose of increasing the knowledge and the effectiveness of workers in their economic and political organizations. It serves simultaneously as a discipline, a directive, and a dynamic.

There are those who question the right of education *of, by,* and *for* the workers to exist and who label its proponents as separatists. Why, they say, make distinctions in education between those who must work for their living and other members of the community? From 1671, when Governor Berkeley of Virginia thanked God that there were "no free schools nor printing," down to modern times when exploiters of southern sharecroppers objected to WPA classes in arithmetic for fear that the sharecroppers would be able to check the deductions made in their accounts, reactionaries have always opposed the extension of education to what they viewed as the "lower classes." Not long ago a prominent representative of big business attacked the University of Michigan Extension Division for running classes in collective bargaining.

In contrast, the support of organized labor for the extension of public education has never faltered during the nineteenth and twentieth centuries. Paradoxically, labor suffers the unique distinction of being a majority which is discriminated against as if it were a minority in the community; and this in public education which labor's support made possible—an attitude that education itself surely should have destroyed by removing the fear and prejudice on which all such discrimination depends.

Workers' education is therefore a necessary recognition of specific needs of an economic group. Curiously enough, special education has been provided for many years—and at government expense— for another large group, the farmers, and no one accuses the rural high schools or the agricultural colleges and the USDA Extension Division of separatism. Too often those who shout separatism are like the drunk who blames the lamp-post for making circles. These semantic antics find a parallel in the insistence by billion-dollar corporation heads that individual private enterprise is the only way to run industry effectively. In one great city the majority of a board of education treated the record in trade union service of a candidate for a position in adult education, as something better to be found on a police blotter. These people are the real working protagonists of separatism. *Our problem is to find, by education, an over-all community pattern for the groups of which the modern community is composed.*

But we should not fool ourselves in thinking that equal educational opportunity already exists for all sections of the community. Only a very relatively small and privileged minority go to college and many students can or cannot go simply because of the size of their papa's bank account. Even the "100 great books" boys forget that thirty-five million Americans live in areas with no library facilities.

Progressive education advocates individualized treatment for each student to find capacities, and adapts courses and teaching to suit. But school teachers must feel such suggestions completely utopian in view of the crowded classrooms they normally have to face. For example, in New York City, in the academic high schools alone, there were 6,845 classes with over forty pupils in 1944. In our nation seventy-five per cent of our adults never completed high school. Ten million adults have never attended school at all.

Despite the fears of the shortsighted reactionaries, education hitherto has been mainly propaganda for the *status quo,* while education about facts indicating the need for social change has usually been dismissed as propaganda. And men do perforce think differently in a palace and in a hut. The toad and the ploughman view the harrow in a different light.

Fortunately, there is now an awakening in our colleges and universities to their responsibilities in training men and women for administrative work and leadership in the trade unions. Outstanding as a cause of this changed attitude of our colleges to organized labor is the great increase in the numerical strength of the unions during the past decade; also the new legal status which the unions enjoy in the community, thanks largely to the Wagner Act.

Nobody worries about education for an Ishmael. When the unions were literally fighting for their lives, the colleges, with a few notable exceptions, also shared in the animosity expressed against them. Too often the colleges trained the economists, the lawyers, the judges, and the business executives who used legal skills to rob injured workers of compensation, justified and practiced the boycott against the unions, granted injunctions against their activities, and developed in the large corporations personnel and welfare work to serve as a backfire against the alleged menace of union organization. Happily, that situation is changing. There is a bridge of mutual assistance being built between the labor unions and the colleges. Already some forty to fifty educational institutions have taken steps in this direction, including the Harvard Union Fellowships and the School of Industrial Relations at Cornell. Extramural work in industrial relations for adults generally is increasing.[3]

[3] See for details and comments *Current History,* October 1944, "Education Discovers Organized Labor"; *American Federationist,* January, 1945, "Higher Education for Labor Leadership?"; *Guidance, Practical Arts and Vocational Education,* January, 1945, "Cap and Gown Meets Overalls"; Caroline Ware, *Labor Education in Universities,* New York, 1946.

Such advances in colleges and for adults will undoubtedly strengthen the trend in grade schools, high schools, and vocational schools to prepare students for life by informing them of the group organization which distinguishes our modern society. Textbooks and courses have shown considerable improvement in recent years, and alert teachers and administrators will welcome and cooperate with such developments.

During wartime, workers' education suffered from the many claims upon the workers' energy. However, there has been a growing variety in projects, with more emphasis upon activity programs and recreational work and less upon formal classes. Some unions run classes for new members. At least two important unions have required courses for would-be full-time officers. In-service training is provided to prevent union officers from becoming mentally muscle-bound.

One new and interesting development has been training of counselors who can function in the shop alongside the shop chairman or steward. The counselor knows all about the social agencies in the community and can answer questions about the price of pork chops as well as where the working mother can find a nursery. During the war, the National CIO War Relief Committee and the War Production Board carried through successful training programs in Detroit, Chicago, and Philadelphia.

This education in overalls does not lend itself to statistical tabulation but it surely plays an important role not only in meeting the needs of the member but in linking him to the educational activities of his union. It will not in any way replace the normal agencies of classroom and teacher for acquiring information.

To the extent that the community and education discover and recognize the needs of labor, to that extent can we secure a mutually beneficial interplay of ideas and cooperation in the provision of facilities. By and large, what is good for labor is good for education and the community.

So far as education in grade school, high school and college goes, the teachers in the American Federation of Teachers and in other progressive teacher groups have done their best to remedy past mistakes. But, as already suggested, we have too often to fill up the dangerous gaps left in our learning before we can proceed to tell the truth about things as they are, things as they have been, and things as they should be, as we defend past advances and build for a better future.

Permit me to make some specific suggestions on what the schools and textbooks should say about trade unionism.

(1) They should give an explanation of the "closed shop" to show that it is no more tyrannical or unfair than our system of public taxation under which the individual cannot escape his contribution to the public revenues, from which he benefits, although in some instances he may not agree with the particular form of the expenditure. As a member of the minority, of course, he has the right to influence the city, state, and federal government to spend the money in a way that would meet with his full approval. Labor itself does not think that the "closed shop" is a blanket method suitable for immediate application to all industries. However, it does insist upon the right of unionists to refuse to work with nonunionists in certain situations, when the latter are enjoying trade union benefits and yet refuse to pay any part of the cost of maintaining them.

(2) The school and the textbook should be at pains to describe the actual functions of the trade union in connection with sick and death benefits, unemployment compensation, and old age pensions. They should give due and proper notice to the apprenticeship system set up by the unions, the enforcement of standards of quality in workmanship, and the cooperation with enlightened employers to help stabilize the industry and to settle all disputed questions by effective mediation procedures.

Teachers should be able to see behind the headlines of newspapers which report strikes on Page 1 and their settlement on Page 20, if at all.[4] They should be able to understand the "lusty imma-

---

[4] An example of newspaper emphasis is seen in the *New York Times,* a journal of high standing. On February 17, 1945, it put on Page 1 a story headed "Radio Head Yields to Petrillo as Having Supremacy in Power," with the carry-over head on Page 9, "Yields to Petrillo as Supreme in U.S." On February 18, it put on Page 32 "U.S. Steel, CIO Sign New Contract; Severance Pay Granted First Time. Agreement Also Includes Conciliation Board to Settle Grievances— Other Firms Are Expected

turity" of unions which have had to fight bitterly to keep alive in previous years and thus lack the experience of collective bargaining which many unions have built up through the years.

All sections of the labor movement regret the jurisdictional disputes which, like other family quarrels, are often fought most bitterly. The labor problems class in school should, however, try to get statements from the groups involved.

(3) The textbooks should also make clear the record about the service given by labor in promoting and maintaining public education from the time of its inception in the United States. They should likewise let the facts of experience speak concerning the results of technological employment upon the workers' standard of life and also the effects of the centralization of power in the hands of the banks and the big corporations, with the resulting dangers of monopoly prices as well as of unemployment.

(4) The textbooks and the school should also examine carefully the role played by the middleman and the speculator who too often escape the censure falling upon high wages as an alleged cause of high prices. The fallacy of the vicious circle in which wage increases are alleged to be the cause of price increases should be carefully examined in the light of the relative movements of wages and prices.

(5) The whole position of labor in society and the importance of its role should be treated with emphasis to help overcome the previous overemphasis upon bookish subjects and academic requirements. The aim would be to show the dignity and importance of both mental and manual labor.

(6) The workers, as the largest group in society, constitute the greatest bloc of consumers. Hence, work in consumer education and consumer cooperatives would be helpful to the trade unions. They would welcome a greater growth in consumer awareness and

---

to Follow Pattern of Pact." Here was the climax of negotiations started in December, 1943, setting a pattern for the major steel corporations and 750,000 organized steel workers. The Page 1 story of the previous day was the protest of a president of a small Minneapolis radio station whose statement happened to confirm an editorial campaign waged by the *New York Times,*

a healthy skepticism about this cosmetic or that laxative as a source of irresistible "oomph" and professional or personal success.

(7) In any examination of wages, annual and life incomes should be stated, not merely hourly rates of pay received by individual workers. This should, of course, be supplemented by a description of the actual conditions under which the high-sounding hourly wage is secured. The absence of social security as a cause of union restrictive rules and "feather-bedding" should be examined.

(8) There should be classes in labor problems in all normal schools and teacher training courses and in the educational departments of all our universities, so that future teachers and writers of textbooks would be able to explain the law of the land concerning collective bargaining. The possibility of applying democratic rights and principles to the workshop should be explored in these courses. If representatives of industry are invited to address school assemblies, then labor people should also be brought in.

In looking at future labor-capital relations, it can be noted that there are three ways by which industry can be carried on, namely, by paternalism, dictatorship, or industrial democracy. The latter involves a recognition that collective bargaining is here to stay; that unions give to groups of otherwise weak individual workers an equality in bargaining strength which is necessary in industry. One of the big new developments in the institutions of higher learning has been, as mentioned already, the recognition that they should help the unions to train their own administrators. The New York Legislature has authorized the School for Industrial and Labor Relations at Cornell as part of this welcome trend.

However much American citizens differ with each other, they all agree that jobs for all are preferable to breadlines. They agree that unemployment means a tremendous loss to the community. Returned soldiers cannot eat medals or service ribbons, and workers are not a stockpile. If the displaced worker and the discontented soldier discover that the community has made no provision for them, we may find that, while fascist forces have been defeated abroad, they may be dangerously present at home.

In the postwar community we should endeavor to provide fifty to eighty million people with full-time employment at decent pay. The war demonstrated that labor-management cooperation can accomplish production miracles. Some four thousand labor-management committees, covering about seven million workers, played a major part in this achievement. If we can continue this cooperation, whatever temporary difficulties may arise, there should be no real obstacle to harnessing our labor force and our tools and workshops to the jobs of meeting the needs of our people and providing adequate employment for our population.

To do this, education is vital to help us re-tool our minds as well as our machines. There is a problem of adjustment, change, and reconversion in our attitudes as well as in our airplane plants and munitions factories. Many of the current plans for the future insist that all the government-owned plants must be handed back to "free enterprise" without any definition of what that phrase really means. Surely we should closely examine "free enterprise" if that means camouflage for corporate monopolies and cartels. A mixed economy, in which public corporations, private business, and collective operation of public services would all play a part, and in which labor, capital, and government cooperate, would be more desirable.

Air Marshal William A. Bishop, V.C., Royal Canadian Air Force, has something to say in his book, *Wingéd Peace,* on this:

The world most people picture seems to be very much like the one we left behind—a world of arrant nationalism and race pride, a world of bitter trade competition and trade barriers. Many people on the North American Continent are raising particular vocal hell *apropos* the merits and demerits of what they call the Free Enterprise system, which seems to be just another phrase to define our old-fashioned capitalist-democracy. Certainly that is not the first question which faces mankind. That first question is whether our civilization is going to survive, or man is going to destroy it; and whether it is to be saved or destroyed through the medium of capitalism or socialism, or a mixture of both, is purely secondary. What I mean is this: If we have not learned from World War II that we dare not fight again, because to fight will mean the annihilation of civilization itself, then what has capitalism on the one hand or conglomerate socialism on the other to do with it? What is the difference between dying of pneumonia or in an airplane crash? Either way a man is dead and that is the first point at issue—the death or the survival of human civilization.

Educators in the social studies have an important role to play in giving an analysis of all social institutions, not forgetting the trade unions in relation to their new role. Education and labor must aid in preparing citizens to face without fear a changing, challenging world. Labor and education, by closer cooperation, can thus shape a better world. Thus the prophecy of Micah shall come to pass to the joy of religion, education, and labor:

> For out of Zion shall go forth the law . . .
> And He shall judge between many peoples,
> And shall decide concerning mighty nations afar off;
> And they shall beat their swords into plowshares,
> And their spears into pruning-hooks;
> Nation shall not lift up sword against nation,
> Neither shall they learn war any more.
> But they shall sit every man under his vine
>   and under his fig-tree;
> And none shall make them afraid.

V

ORGANIZED LABOR AND POLITICS

BY

DWIGHT J. BRADLEY

Former Director, Religious Associates, National Citizens Political Action Committee

The orthodox pattern for organized labor in this country, in relation to action in politics, was laid down during the period between 1900 and the First World War under the influence of Samuel Gompers and his associates in the American Federation of Labor. It was defined with almost classic simplicity by the phrase—"We punish our enemies and reward our friends."

Like all other orthodoxies, this doctrine could gain general acceptance only after much argument and conflict. From the beginning of labor's slow and painful progress, two major schools of thought and two tendencies had contested for dominance in the political approach. The one, conscious of difficulties in the way of achieving and maintaining political power sufficient to satisfy the workers' social and economic claims and unwilling to be identified with a socialist or other politically left wing program, advocated a restriction of labor's action to purely economic fields, except when it was possible to help elect a friendly candidate or to defeat a hostile one, or to put pressure on legislative bodies in behalf of this or that specific labor-supported measure.

The other approach was that of direct political action, which, while not sacrificing the economic weapons of the strike, the closed shop, and collective bargaining, counseled full participation in politics even to the point of organizing a Labor Party or of joining forces with socialist and other left wing movements of a definitely political character. Under the influence of Samuel Gompers, American labor was constrained to follow the nonpolitical course, but only after the failure of a series of abortive efforts to enroll the unions in organizations with definitely political aims.

Organized labor was, until very recently, without accepted status in the United States as a whole. Many who come from nonlabor backgrounds can remember how, in their childhood, they were taught to regard unions as being not only socialistic and dangerous but actually evil and satanic—things to be hated and fought against by all good people, and especially by members of churches. It was contended, also, that "fine, respectable working people" should be protected in every possible way, even by calling out the militia if necessary, against the machinations of "wicked" organizers with their "un-American theories" and their "subversive tendencies." The names of Eugene V. Debs, Daniel De Leon, "Bill" Haywood, and John L. Lewis, along with that of Samuel Gompers, were held up to innocent little children and to budding youth as fearful examples of what "atheistic socialism" or downright anarchy could do to destroy the values of true civilization.

In such a setting and, furthermore, in view of the deepseated antipathy of the large majority of the American electorate to any third party movement of any sort, it may have been the part of wisdom for labor at that stage to abstain from political action except as a kind of guerrilla warfare. The primary task of a union was, and is, to help the working man get better wages and shorter hours, to improve the conditions under which he works and, collaterally, to make it possible for him to live in better houses, wear better clothes, eat better food, and provide his children with opportunities for higher education and a more abundant life. The labor movement has striven from the first to give those who were exploited, dispossessed, and ignored by industrial civilization a chance to share in the major benefits of a rising standard of living. Being relatively powerless, as individuals, to withstand the forces arrayed against them, the working people joined into unions to fight as best they could for what they had every reason to consider their just rights. The economic weapons seemed most available and most effective. The political weapon seemed to prove, after several experiments, far less so. Thus, the Gompers tradition established itself in the American labor movement as a whole, retaining its authority until the great crisis of 1935 in labor history, when the Committee for Industrial Organization was set up.

During the first six years after the founding of the CIO, the labor movement in the United States underwent a profound change. The membership greatly increased, not only in the new unions, but also in those affiliated with the American Federation of Labor. With the encouragement of the Roosevelt Administration and through its positive support, an entirely fresh approach to the question of labor's participation in the nation's life commenced to be taken for granted by everyone except those who steadfastly refused to recognize and to accept the new era. The Wagner Act was passed and signed by the President, giving labor a legal status never before enjoyed, and providing for safeguards, advantages, and a position before the law, such as labor had hitherto striven for at great effort but with only indifferent success. For the first time in the nation's history, the labor movement had a friend in the White House and supporters in Congress, determined to provide that organized labor should receive an understanding and a recognition for which it had hitherto struggled alone, much of the time against the apathy or the hostility of government.

Under the stimulation of John L. Lewis, there was organized in 1936 a movement for political action within the ranks of labor, known as Labor's Non-Partisan League. This marked the first step away from the orthodox Gompers position and toward a consistent and realistic approach to politics as a means of achieving legitimate union objectives. But this movement did not carry over beyond the first flush of its success, and commenced to fade with the liberalization of the Supreme Court and the passage of the Wagner Fair Labor Practices Act. By the time of the national election in 1940, it had, to all intents and purposes, ceased to be. Whatever may have been the specific forces that caused its disintegration—one of which was, obviously, the split within the CIO and the withdrawal of John L. Lewis and the United Mine Workers—the underlying cause was the failure sufficiently to recognize that political action requires constant, expert, organized effort to develop, in the public mind, habitual attitudes that will impel citizens to study issues as a prelude to voting on election day.

The 1942 election, the smallest for years in number of ballots cast, resulted in a negative triumph for antilabor reaction. It was negative because the election, from labor's standpoint, was lost by default. Organized labor, in 1936 and again in 1940, had proved its strength in helping to make possible the re-election of Roosevelt to his second and his third terms. It had helped to place in Congress a working majority of Representatives and Senators who, whatever their private convictions, could be counted on to go down the line behind the President in his progressive policies. But after 1942 the atmosphere changed. Congress was no longer responsive to liberal or progressive stimulations. A coalition of anti-New Deal Democrats and conservative, ultrapartisan Republicans placed the balance of power in the hands of those who regarded organized labor as an enemy. Passage of the Smith-Connolly Act was a symbol. An entire social philosophy was summed up in its motivation and in its objectives.

It was in view of this situation that, in 1943, the leaders of the CIO came together to plan a program to counteract the reactionary trends which, largely through apathy and neglect, had dominated the election the year before. These leaders were aware of the close connection between a small vote and a disastrous result. They realized that, if the people as a whole stayed away from the polls, there was more likelihood that the minority who went to the polls would be, in large proportion, conservative, and that, therefore, those who were antagonistic to the interests of organized labor, as well as to progressive action in general, would elect their candidates with slight opposition.

The meeting to set up an effective movement to counteract reaction was called by Philip Murray, president of the CIO. It was held in July, a few months more than a year before the crucial election of 1944. At this meeting, Mr. Murray declared, "For the first time in American history, the forces of labor are now setting up a nationwide organization to protect the political rights of the working man as well as the rights of the returning soldier, the farmer, the small businessman, and the so-called 'common man.' "

This statement by Mr. Murray is noteworthy for the fact that it indicated two lines of advance beyond previous attitudes on the part of organized labor in the United States toward political action. In the first place, labor here announced that it was entering politics on a permanent basis, through "a nationwide organization to protect the *political* rights of the working man. . . ." In the second place, labor here affirmed its interest in the rights of those outside its own ranks —"the returning soldier, the farmer, the small businessman, and the so-called 'common man.' "

Not since Samuel Gompers established the orthodox American labor doctrine of essentially hit-or-miss participation in politics, by "rewarding our friends and punishing our enemies," had any outstanding and responsible leaders of the labor movement publicly proposed to lead their unions into any organization of a distinctly political character with specifically political aims. Labor's Non-Partisan League had tended in this direction, but had not taken the final step. Because it had not taken this final step, it could not overcome the effects of factionalism within its own body. Because it had paused at the threshold of true political action, it had not been able to grasp its greatest opportunity in a time when the course of history was being shaped far more surely on the political level than on that of purely economic conflict and advance. Because it had halted, it had failed—and by its failure had opened the way to a potential failure of the entire program so successfully begun in 1936.

It is even more significant that, in his statement of July, 1943, Mr. Murray placed the new organization on the side of *all* Americans who are struggling for the advancement of the people as a whole, on the side of those men and women in every walk of life whose outlook, attitudes, and interests extend toward the future, and who are convinced that they have more to gain than to lose as society develops more democratic ways of living in the cultural, economic, and political areas where all have a common stake.

In other words, for the first time, the progressive labor movement made common cause politically with other movements and groups. No longer were the unions fighting a lone battle against the dominating forces of the country; rather they asserted that between themselves and the farmers, the professional people, the returning service men and women, the small businessmen and progressives of every vocation, there is a great common denominator of mutual interest.

The orthodox practice had been to enter politics only when it was thought that politics could be economically useful—could be turned to the special advantage of the trade unions in some particular way: through a favorable plank in a party platform, through the election of friendly candidates, through the ousting of officials with bad labor records, through certain pieces of prolabor legislation. As a general policy, politics was left to the politicians; and these were usually looked upon with hostility or contempt. Political action itself was something to be avoided if possible, and got into only if necessary.

Under the leadership of Philip Murray and Sidney Hillman, however, the more positive democratic concept was introduced. To the CIO Political Action Committee, politics was something to be entered with sagacity and circumspection, not grudgingly as a last resort and not merely as a means to special ends. Without abandoning its own economic weapons, to be used in cases of necessity, or giving up its legislative and elective procedures long since established to gain definite labor objectives, the CIO, through its Political Action Committee, extended the scope of its interest and the areas of its responsibility to take in all Americans irrespective of status, vocation, creed, race, or national origin.

While the CIO-PAC was still hardly under way, it ran into difficulties arising out of the division within the labor movement. The question arose, naturally, as to whether, in such an ambitious project as this, the American Federation of Labor and other great bodies, such as the Railway Brotherhoods and the United Mine Workers, might decide to make common cause with the CIO. As it turned out, the A. F. of L. leadership refused to come in, partly because most of the unions of this group adhere, at least officially, to the Gompers tradition. Mr. Lewis, for personal reasons if for no other, would permit the United Mine Workers to have nothing to do with the movement. The Railway Brotherhoods remained officially aloof.

In no way abashed, however, the CIO, knowing its own great strength, went ahead—believing that the rank and file of the labor movement, whether of the CIO or not, would join in this new step toward solving the problems of the workingman through full participation in the political life of the nation.

The first task was to get out the vote. Since it had become apparent that there is a close connection between a small vote and a reactionary, or at least conservative, result, it was also plain that, if the people will only exercise their franchise, they can control political trends. If the myriads who live "on the wrong side of the tracks," in the small apartments, in the housing projects, in the workers' districts, in the segregated sections, in tenements and out on the farms, will register and go to the polls—if the citizens who have never enjoyed a fair return upon the investments they have made in our industrial civilization, will express their will on election day—they can outvote the powerful but infinitesimal minority of those who thus far have received the richest share of our national wealth. This is, obviously, the democratic way to achieve social progress, the way provided in our Constitution. To recognize its possibilities indicates good judgment.

On this assumption, the CIO-PAC went to work to get the people politically aroused. Six months before the election in 1944, no one would have dared predict that it would be a great election from the standpoint of popular participation. The campaign plans of political strategists, unfriendly to organized labor and to social progress in general, were developed on the theory that the political apathy of 1942 would continue, at least for the duration of the war. The Gallup Poll, which commenced by predicting a total popular vote of not more than eighteen million, was driven finally to admit that it might reach the figure of twenty-six million—and even then fell short of the mark actually made.

Counteracting with a strategy of their own, the PAC planners proceeded to stimulate enthusiasm for widespread registration of all eligible voters. The workers went out in droves, ringing door-bells, distributing tracts and pamphlets, urging everyone to prepare for full participation in the crucial business of government on November 7. The re-election of President Roosevelt and the election of a progressive Congress were the two major objectives; but there were also local issues of hardly less importance.

The people were awakened. It was not long before the conservative opposition also began working up a large vote, realizing that if the progressives were the only ones active in this field, the chances of electing any of their own candidates would be slim. This meant an almost complete reversal of policy, since the earlier planning had built the campaign on electoral apathy. What is more, the conservatives tried, with increasing desperation, to present themselves as being the real and true progressives; for they came to see that, with the probability of a big vote, a campaign based only on reactionary or antiprogressive appeals would not succeed. The apparent confusion of the Republican campaign was due, almost entirely, to the necessity of holding all the backward looking voters on the one hand, and of drawing in, by political pretense, as many as they could of those who sincerely wished for a forward looking administration.

As a byproduct, therefore, of the distinctly progressive effort to get to the polls all who would vote for the program of the CIO-PAC, the entire electorate, both liberal and conservative, became politically alive. Whatever a critic may say in condemnation of the CIO-PAC program, he must, if he has the basic interest of America at heart, be grateful to it for having brought to bear such a stimulating influence upon the electorate at so important a time.

The question is raised, now and then, as to whether political action constitutes a legitimate activity of labor unions. It has always been answered in the negative by those who follow the orthodox line of Samuel Gompers. Is this, then, a case of the unions stepping outside their proper role and entering a field where they have no business to go? As a practical matter, the answer depends on how one defines the terms of political action in a democracy such as ours.

If one is convinced that political action should be confined to the official parties, as a kind of special profession, and that other groups and organizations should work only as pressure groups or as lobbies, he must admit that the labor movement has no business to go into politics as the CIO-PAC and the National Citizens PAC did.

It would mean, in other words, that only within the already constituted parties, or perhaps within a third party or a fourth, would it be proper for American citizens to express themselves politically, except in sporadic ways. It would mean, further, that if citizens join an organization outside a political party, they must see to it that this organization does not function as a political movement.

This appears, on the face of it, to be an entirely arbitrary point of view and one which, if carried to its logical end, would be instrumental in developing even further the tendency to promote hidden political interests under the camouflage of a false "nonpolitical" front. Politics in a democracy must be open. Otherwise it degenerates into a series of intrigues.

The party system in America grew up, informally at first, to meet a specific need: the need for organizations to cultivate, promulgate, and get into effect certain special convictions shared by numbers of citizens. There is nothing in our Constitution which calls for a party system. George Washington, in his Farewell Address, warned his fellow countrymen against the dangers of partisanship, indicating his fear lest a party system should develop. It "grew up like Topsy" because of the necessities of the situation, and then became so deeply integrated in our political existence as to be, to all intents and purposes, ineradicable.

What is more, the two-party system seems to have established itself so firmly that no third party movement has, thus far at least, been able to survive beyond the first flush of enthusiasm. Either the newer party eliminates and absorbs one of the older parties, or it quickly liquidates itself. Whenever a third party has arisen under the aspiring leadership of a genius like Robert LaFollette, Sr., or Theodore Roosevelt, it has come a certain distance and then fallen back. When its leader disappeared or lost interest, it disappeared and its members lost interest. Yet the old parties continue, despite their innumerable inner contradictions or possibly because they are able to contain so many contradictions within a continuing structure of loyalty and general interest.

One wonders, however, how the party system in this country is to be revitalized and made germane to the present and the future. Political organization has seemed, in recent years, to have grown moribund: yet a great new sensitivity to political issues, a great new desire for the integrity of party platforms, party practices, and party objectives, has taken hold of millions of hitherto disinterested citizens. At the present time, indeed, the so-called "independent voter," who holds the balance of political power in America, is looking for some more definite and effective affiliation through which he may work as a responsible participant in the ongoing life of the nation. Most idealists, with the exception of the relatively small number who have joined the Socialist Party or another of the more progressive political organizations with platforms and candidates of their own, chafe at the slowness, the willingness to compromise, the bossism, and the reactionary drift in the parties which muster the largest following. The intellectuals, the religious liberals, the politically scrupulous, and most progressives are usually contemptuous, if not bitter, in their attitude toward present-day American politics. To them, the party system has itself become outmoded: outmoded because it has seemed to have so little life within itself. Platforms are taken seriously by few, and these few are commonly the naïve.

If, then, the party system is to continue without being merely the instrumentality of the corrupt and the self-seeking, how may it be rehabilitated? How may it become once more the vehicle of an honest, intelligent, and forward looking American democracy? By another effort to set up a third party? Those initially responsible for the organization and program of the PAC answered in a simple negative. They had definitely made up their minds from the beginning that no third party movement should be permitted to draw them aside from the main objectives, which were not the establishment of a party but the introduction into the present political structures of a fresh, vigorous, and progressive force which might save the two major parties from dying of dry rot. Despite the fact that

Sidney Hillman, Chairman of the PAC, was an organizer of the American Labor Party in New York and remained as its Chairman until his death, he himself was most determined that the PAC should become neither the nucleus nor main resource of a new party, nor an affiliate of the American Labor Party, nor a mere agent of either of the major parties. In other words, the CIO-PAC and the National Citizens PAC (which was organized in 1944 as an extension of the PAC program into the broader field of nonlabor citizenry) established and maintained through the 1944 campaign and election the principle of true nonpartisanship.

The representatives of the CIO-PAC went to the Democratic and Republican Conventions to present their case. The Republican Party was only mildly interested in what the PAC proposed. The Democratic Party was greatly interested. In fact, a whole mythology grew out of this interest, culminating in the well-known and seriously misrepresented saying, "Clear it with Sidney."

It is not a myth, however, that the Democratic platform builders were more concerned with what the CIO-PAC had to offer than were those who prepared the Republican planks. This was the result of the seasoned sagacity of the Democratic politicos who could understand a handwriting on the wall which, to the Republicans at that early stage in the campaign, made little sense. The Republican strategists, during the summer of 1944, did not think that the CIO-PAC would cut much ice politically and, in fact, had so slight an opinion of its political potency that they went out of their way at first to build it up in order that, at the proper time, they could coolly knock it down. They failed in this enterprise; and one might reasonably have supposed that, before another campaign had got under way, the Republicans would have been hard at work to gain the support of organized labor, since labor had shown itself to be a major factor in American politics.

President Roosevelt's prestige was, of course, of enormous influence in the 1944 election. Liberals and progressives of all parties went down the line for Roosevelt because of his foreign policy and his leadership in the war. All liberals wished, also, to have progressives in Congress, though the results were disappointing, as has been proved by the trend of affairs in the Senate and House in 1945 and 1946.

The entrance of the PAC into the political arena in 1943-44 gave new life and, meaning not only to the liberal movement in America, but also to the party system itself. By stirring business elements, along with professional and scientific and artistic groups, to set up their own voluntary political action organizations, the PAC served as an over-all agent for the entire progressive tendency in our nation.

We have entered an era in which, more than for many decades, political action is the primary responsibility of those who are zealous to carry on into cultural and economic areas the democratic way of life—to build on new and stronger foundations the democratic institutions shaken by the depression and the war. Political action, in simplest terms, is the way the people of a democracy keep the government as their instrument, refusing to let it become their ruler or the instrument of an *élite;* the way in which they make concrete their wishes, their demands, and their ideals in legislation, in administration, and through the courts.

VI

DISCRIMINATION AGAINST MINORITIES

BY

A. PHILIP RANDOLPH

*International President, Brotherhood of Sleeping Car Porters,
A. F. of L.*

I want to discuss in this article a few general propositions in relation to the question of minorities. One is that the question of race and color has become the central social issue of these times. There are several reasons for this: two thirds of the peoples of the world are peoples of color; the peoples of color have risen to a higher level of moral, spiritual, and intellectual maturity; the Axis forces have stressed the question of a master race more violently and methodically than the world has ever witnessed before; and the ideologies advocated by Nietzsche, Bismarck, Bernhardi, Count de Gobineau, Houston Chamberlain, Thomas Dixon, and others, have gained wide circulation among the peoples of the world. Another important fact: the peoples of color today are in revolt against the idea of the master race. This is true virtually everywhere.

While we may not designate India as a minority purely from the point of view of color, nevertheless because it is an oppressed country it should fall within the general category of a minority. Here you have an outstanding example of revolt against a great world power, the British Empire, and an extraordinary exemplification of spiritual sacrifice on the part of the leaders in order that they may be able to win and achieve freedom and independence for India.

We heard much about the clashing of the tanks of Rommel and Montgomery in North Africa, and about the intrigues of Darlan, Giraud, and De Gaulle; but we did not hear much about the struggles of the people there for independence and their revolt for freedom. The Berbers, Jews, Negroes, and Arabs in North Africa are not satisfied even under so-called free France, for there are still some seventy million people of color under the dominion of that government.

South of the Sahara Desert there are multitudes of Negroes, one hundred million or more, and, while nobody hears very much about what they are doing, they, too, are stirring with revolt against the domination by white power nations they have experienced throughout the years.

We know that in the Union of South Africa there is a dangerous condition because the black natives are not given ordinary opportunities to share in the democratic processes of government. The great international statesman, Marshal Jan Christian Smuts, has done practically nothing to integrate these black natives into the democratic machinery of the government of South Africa. It is preeminently known as the land of the color bar and the pass law. Because of the fear of engulfment of some two or more million whites in a sea of eight or more million blacks, South African white leaders are fervent advocates of the theories of Nazi racialism. Native blacks are excluded from participation in the national, provincial, and municipal governments. The South African parliament has two hundred members, all white, seven of whom are designated to represent the blacks.

In the West Indies, the Bahamas, Jamaica, and Trinidad, the natives have staged mass job-wage riots in the recent past. The natives have struck in their attempt to secure higher wages from the plantation owners. They have also burned down some plantations of sugar cane, indicating their discontent with the economic conditions prevailing there.

In America also, there exists in the hearts of the Negro people a burning desire for a transformation from the status of second-class to first-class citizenship. Black Americans are on the march. They seek complete equality, economic, political, and social.

Let me observe that the problem of minorities is fundamentally the problem of discrimination and segregation. We find manifestations of this segregation and discrimination in various areas of life.

On the railroads we have the Jim Crow car. This peculiar form of segregation applies almost entirely to Negroes. Incidentally, the Supreme Court has taken the position, strangely enough, that segregation is not discrimination when there are so-called equal accommodations.

One young Negro, who experimented with the principle of non-violent direct action against Jim Crow on the railroads, went into the lounge car on one of the through trains from New York to Miami, and was told to get out. He said, "No, I am not going to get out, because the Supreme Court has said that equal accommodations must be provided for people without regard to color, religion, race, or nationality. If you don't want me in this lounge car, then put another car on this train for me." Of course, the conductor was greatly distressed and befuddled. Finally, this young Negro was let alone, and remained in the lounge car.

A number of absurd and preposterous conditions exist because of these absurd forms of discrimination and segregation. On the buses throughout the South, you have the Jim Crow system in intrastate travel. It is interesting to observe the spiritual injury that is done to the young Negro. I was in San Antonio some time ago and a colored lad of about five years of age got on the bus and went straight to the rear. No one said anything to him. Then a young white boy got on the bus, and he sat right up in the front. Here you have a spiritual situation that fairly kills the soul of the young Negro boy, who feels that he must go to the rear because he is alleged to be different and inferior.

The Jim Crow system is a sharp and shameful insult to the soul of the Negro people all over America and is designed to break their spirit. On the boats operating between Jacksonville and New York, Negroes cannot purchase first-class accommodations. They must remain in the bottom of the boat until they are ready to disembark. They are not even permitted to look at the ocean from the deck of the ship.

In the theaters, we have the same problem of segregation and discrimination. In certain parts of the South, Negroes are not permitted to attend any theater, and in others they are given the opportunity to sit in what they call the "Roost." It is opprobriously labeled, "Jim-Crow Roost."

Also, we have these forms of discrimination in all types of entertainment and amusement. I was in Toronto a few years ago when a group of young Negro boys and girls demanded the right to attend the dance halls when the Negro name bands came to the city. They got together with some of the young white boys and girls of one of the churches and planned to picket the dance hall that had discriminated against them. When the city officials found out that this was being discussed, they called them in and said, "Now, we are going to see to it that you get the privilege of going to the dance halls when Duke Ellington, or Cab Calloway, or any Negro band comes to the city." The young Negro boys and girls accepted it. They thought they had been given a tremendous concession. So they made an agreement to attend when the Negro bands came to town.

Later on when I was in Toronto they consulted me concerning the matter. I said, "Why, you have done violence to the principle of racial equality. You must go back and tell the city officials that you want to exercise your right as citizens to attend any dance hall at any time, and that you do not want to be the victims of segregation." They saw the point and promptly changed their strategy and set to work on this problem.

We also have manifestations of discrimination in books. When I was in City College in New York, I was in a class where we talked about *The Passing of the Great Race,* by Madison Grant. I remember in that class there was an attempt to emphasize the inferiority of certain groups, certain races. I recall the suggestion made by the professor that there are certain races that are incapable of sustained intellectual application because they are superemotional. Into that category, Negroes were placed. I was but a youngster, but I resented it and protested against it, and from that hour on I was a sort of *persona non grata* in the class.

We have in the literature of the country many books and publications that disseminate the doctrine of racial inferiority. I do not know a single history in the public schools or colleges in America that scientifically, properly, and adequately portrays the role of the Negro people in this country, or, for that matter, the roles of the Jew, Catholic, or foreigner.

We have discrimination and segregation practiced by certain of the big, reputable colleges and universities. This is true without exception in the South, of course, but it has been hardly less true in the remainder of the nation. Some slight improvement was gained under college training provided by the armed forces during the war, but the situation remains largely discriminatory. In certain colleges where Negroes are permitted to enter, they are not allowed to have free access to the dormitory facilities. This is true in virtually all of the big colleges, so this problem of discrimination on account of race, color, religion, national origin, or ancestry is rather sharp in the realm of education. Jews, Italians, Catholics, and Negroes are limited to certain quotas by certain colleges and universities in the free state and city of New York.

Race discrimination and the ideas of segregation are disseminated through the movies. I do not know a single movie that gives a dignified picture of the life of the Negro. They depict the Negro in the role of a clown, giving him ridiculous parts, showing him as being afraid of ghosts, etc.

On the radio, we have Amos and Andy who hold the Negro up to fun and ridicule, by making much over Negro businessmen operating a fresh-air taxi. This is a subtle form of propaganda that makes people feel that Negro businessmen are a joke. If Negroes are considered funny, if they are regarded as clowns, then they are presumably not yet ready for any serious thought or the status of first-class citizens.

The press is perhaps one of the most powerful agencies in developing a discriminatory attitude toward the Negro people in particular. If a Negro boy, for instance, steals an apple, daily papers say, "A Negro boy stole an apple." If a white boy, or an Italian boy, or a boy of any other nationality steals an apple, the press says, "A boy stole an apple." The public mind is conditioned by this kind of reporting because the public comes to associate the stealing of an apple with a Negro boy.

All of us perhaps have heard of the experience of a Russian psychologist who held a piece of beef up before a dog sixty or seventy times, and each time rang a bell, whereupon saliva flowed from the mouth of the dog. As a result of this repetition of holding the beef before the dog and contemporaneously ringing the bell, he did not have to hold up the beef; just the ringing of the bell caused saliva to flow from the dog's mouth. Here was a process of conditioning the flowing of the saliva of the dog by associating beef with a bell.

The mind of the public is being conditioned on race, religion, and nationality. Hitler did this. Look what happened to the world. It is not strange that there should be adverse reactions by the public when the rights of minority groups are raised. The youngster in the home is the victim of psychological suggestions that a Negro is inferior, or that a Jew is a cheater, or that a Catholic is hypocritical. When the child goes out of his home and gives expression to the prejudices that have been built into his consciousness as the result of these psychological suggestions, some people will say that white children are born hating black people. But this is not so. Hatreds are acquired. They are not innate.

We have also the problem of discrimination and segregation in housing. In a large number of the metropolitan centers we have covenants, entered into by various groups of citizens, that are designed to restrict the Negro to certain sections. This operates not only to increase the rent that Negroes have to pay over and above the general level, but also brings about congestion and delinquency, and so forth. When there is increased delinquency, the Negro is pointed out as being more criminal than other people. He is denied housing, he is restricted to certain centers, and then some sociologist comes around and makes a survey and reaches the conclusion that by virtue of race there are certain criminal tendencies among this particular group of people, when actually the bad social conditions create criminals.

In Chicago the restriction of the Negro to certain areas has become a threatening condition, and the time will come when it will be more threatening in New York, and in every other city that works on this unsound and dangerous social principle of the segregation of peoples because of color, race, or religion.

Perhaps the most serious form of segregation and discrimination that the minorities face is in the field of employment. Today we have what are known as white men's jobs. For instance, engineering is a white man's job, and telephone-operating is a white girl's job. Because of this there are wide areas of employment from which Negroes are absolutely excluded. Therefore you have the problem of the Negro people securing work with which to secure wages to buy food, clothing, and shelter. This is the most serious problem of all.

For a long time Negroes were not supposed to enter the field of public utilities, except as porters, and it was not until the Negroes themselves rose up with drastic action, in the form of picketing and actually turning over buses, that Negroes were permitted to operate the buses here in New York. That was a rather violent procedure, but no action was taken until masses of Negroes stopped the buses in New York City, a place which is supposed to be relatively democratic in spirit. The same thing was true in other cities. Of special interest also is the question of employment in the railroad industry.

Perhaps the most interesting approach to this question came about when the national defense program began and the white people on relief were being taken off and given jobs in defense industries, while Negroes were forced to remain on relief. Negroes went around to various industries, begging for work, and they were given the run-around! They were told, "We have never hired Negroes in this industry." Especially was that the case in the airplane industry.

This thing became so serious that a sense of defeatism and desperation seized the hearts of young Negroes all over the country. Some of them became cynical and pessimistic. They went to the YMCA's and YWCA's, churches, and the unions and said, "We have got to work, we want to work, and we are being denied the right to work. We want to help build ships; we want to help win the war." The unions had their closed shops, and the Negroes were told, "Nobody can work here unless he is a member of the union." When they went around to get a card from the union to join, they were told, "You can't get a union card until you have got a job." So there was the vicious circle.

Because of this condition, some Negro leaders came together and started a movement to get the President to take action. They went to the White House and talked to President Roosevelt. President Roosevelt was an amiable person, very polite, with a rare and charming personality, and inclined to lend you his ear. They talked to him at length, and in every instance he said, "Yes, discrimination is wrong. Negroes must have the opportunity to work in these defense industries." And Negroes would go away, and nothing would happen.

So they decided that the conferences held were perhaps not effective, and they started a nationwide movement to march on Washington. Evidently the FBI got around in various parts of the country, and found out that the Negroes were in earnest about it, and were really going to march on Washington. A few weeks before the Negroes were to march, President Roosevelt called the group in again and talked about this question. He had some of his top Cabinet people there and they talked at length. When the Negro leaders were ready to go, they said, "Well, Mr. President, just before we leave we want to leave this impression with you, and that is that the Negroes throughout the country are discontented with the way they are being treated during this crisis. They want to work, they feel they have got the right to work, and unless the Negroes get work, they are going to march on Washington."

President Roosevelt said, "We are going to see that Negroes get work." Then he said, "I want all of the people in this conference to go into my Cabinet room and stay there until you find some remedy to this situation."

In the Cabinet room, Mr. Stimson served as the chairman, and there the Negro leaders, Cabinet members and other government officials talked and talked and talked. Finally they created a subcommittee, and out of it all came Executive Order 8802, under which the President's Committee on Fair Employment Practice was established. This committee did remarkable work. It was able to get Negroes into a large number of industries.

The problem of upgrading Negroes on the basis of their skill is serious. In the Packard plant in Detroit, for example, 24,000 workers walked out when a half-dozen Negroes were upgraded to higher-skilled jobs. The Negroes were driven out of jobs in Mobile, Alabama, by sheer physical violence, because a few were given skilled jobs. The same thing happened in Beaumont, Texas. But the President's Committee on Fair Employment Practice worked diligently, and, as a result of the procedures it adopted, it was able to integrate the Negroes into many industries throughout the country.

Despite the defeat in Congress of the bill for a permanent FEPC, and the subsequent liquidation of the existing agency, there is a spirit and feeling on the part of a large number of people that the Fair Employment Practice Committee should be permanent. A national council for a permanent FEPC was formed and went to work. I believe that the passage of this bill would do much to make the economic lot of the minorities hopeful and promising.

It is also important to observe discrimination and segregation as practiced by the federal government itself. It is recognized today that there is no supervisory work done by Negroes, except over Negroes, in the federal government. Practically all Negro supervisors are segregated, so the federal government itself is perpetuating the pattern of segregation in relation to the Negro people. The problem of democratizing the government so that it will recognize its obligation to deal fairly with its own citizens, is one of the biggest questions that confront us.

Segregation and discrimination in the trade unions are two of the knottiest of all questions. There are twenty or more unions affiliated with the American Federation of Labor that have color clauses prohibiting Negroes from becoming members. There are some unions that do not have color clauses but practice discrimination against Negroes just the same. There are some unions in which Negroes are given the privilege to pay dues, although they have neither voice nor vote in determining policies. They are auxiliary unions. This is a rather subtle device that some of the international unions have developed, so that they can boast that they do not keep Negroes out of their organizations entirely. They give them the right of taxation without representation. It is interesting to know that some of the people in the high command of the American Federation of Labor think that is perfectly all right. Nor is the CIO any lily of trade union purity in this matter. While the CIO leaders like the A. F. of L. leaders condemn racial discrimination, the members of the rank and file in some plants strike against skilled Negro workers. When you get some union leaders to discuss the question, they say, "We must move along gradually on the theory of education. We must take gradual steps." So, according to their theory, we will have no steps taken against discrimination by some of the unions for an astronomical period of time. This, of course, is condemned by the Negro people. But it is only objective to say that progress is being made by the A. F. of L. and the CIO in integrating Negro workers into the labor movement.

In the field of politics, we have discrimination as practiced through the poll tax. The poll tax does not disfranchise Negro workers only, but white workers as well. Even if we were able to eliminate the poll tax, that would not necessarily mean that Negroes would vote. Congressman Rankin has stated that we may abolish the poll tax tomorrow, and not one Negro in Mississippi will vote. Through registration devices, Negroes, when they go to the poll, are given the run-around. They are told to come back four or five times, to disgust and inconvenience them. It does not make any difference if a prospective Negro voter is an M.A. or a Ph.D.; it does not help him at the polls in Dixie. Today, there is a change. The United States Supreme Court decision declaring white primaries illegal brought it about. Now, Negroes are voting all over the South, although there is still opposition.

Segregation in the Armed Forces perhaps touches the Negro more sharply than anything else. I believe the fact that we have discrimination and segregation in the Armed Forces gives rise to race tension and riots perhaps more than any other single thing. For instance, Negro boys in Uncle Sam's uniform, when traveling between certain camps in the South, cannot eat in the diner; they must wait until they reach camp, or they must get a sandwich or a cup of coffee from the butcher boy.

In certain sections, the very presence of a Negro in uniform seems to provoke racial antipathy. Negro boys in uniform are put upon and beaten up. In certain instances they have been shot and lynched. These things rankle in the hearts and minds of the Negro people. We have two armies in America: we have U.S.A. army "first-class" and white, and U.S.A. army "second-class," colored. This is the essence of racism. We sent to Europe two armies which represented our support of Nazi theories of racialism to fight to overthrow Hitlerism. What a contradiction!

Today the Negro people are concerned with securing a federal proclamation for the abolition of segregation and discrimination in the Armed Forces. There are some who say, "Well, now, you can't expect the millennium overnight, and therefore you must depend upon the processes of education. Suppose a proclamation abolishing Jim Crow in the Armed Forces were issued and Army officers refused to observe it?" Let us first have such a proclamation issued, and then deal with the consequences. I believe they would observe it.

At the top of the remedies that we suggest is the organization of the Negro into the labor movement. The labor movement is a place where people fight for common improvements, and when they fight together for these improvements, they come to find they are not so very different after all, that their points of difference are not as sharp as their points of general and common interest. Consequently, it is apparent to the peoples who are included among the minorities that the labor movement represents the most potent and effective force in bringing about greater cooperation among the workers and the eventual abolition of discrimination and segregation.

Our next remedy is legislative. We believe that a National Racial Practices Act should be enacted. It is said that we cannot erase prejudice out of the hearts and minds of people by law, but you can stop mobs from lynching Negroes. We can, by legislation, stop hoodlums and vandals from desecrating synagogues and cathedrals.

We can also give Negroes the right to employment. The fight for the National Labor Relations Act, the National Railroad Act, the Railway Labor Act, the Wages and Hours Act and subsequent legislation, was an effective and potent form of education. Moreover, education ought to be centered around some central and crucial economic, political, and social issue. We may say that we want to educate the people to understand that they should work together, and that they should not resort to violence because of various prejudices, but there must be something concrete around which to build this type of education. An act known as a National Racial Practices Act seems to me to be something concrete that can be used to educate the people and break down and stop discrimination. It may not eliminate race prejudice, but it may stop discrimination and segregation.

As I said before, we are working toward the enactment of a Fair Employment Practices Act. The prospects are that this piece of legislation will eventually be effective in breaking down barriers against minorities.

Some of us have also sought to get the President to appoint a national commission on race. We believe that such a commission, well complemented with sociologists, anthropologists, economists, historians, and psychologists, could explore the whole question of the minorities. Upon the basis of scientific study and survey, we then would be able to work out the processes, strategies, and methods that may be helpful and effective in eliminating segregation and discrimination against minorities.

We have never had a commission of this sort. Nobody has ever seriously attacked this problem realistically. Hence, if the President can be persuaded to appoint such a commission, composed of people outstanding in science, labor, and business, as well as of people with general public interest representative of all America, we will be able to move along a constructive path for the elimination of the tension and conflicts incident to the existence of antagonisms and hostilities against minorities.

Mayor Kelly of Chicago and Governor Green of Illinois appointed such commissions, and there is a rapidly growing number of similar bodies in the country.

The Negroes have developed another technique to meet the problem of discrimination in public places, and that is nonviolent, goodwill direct action. It is not a version of Indian nonviolent action; it is wholly different. As a matter of fact, it is practiced by both white and colored people. When Negroes go into a place where they are denied service, they request a conference with the manager. White friends, who have gone in ahead of the Negroes, then step forward and indicate their interest in the matter. If the manager refuses to listen to the protests, there may be resort to picketing the place, or to a sit-down strike. Techniques vary in accordance with the particular situation.

We used this method in dealing with hotels and restaurants in Chicago. About fifty restaurants in Chicago that denied service to Negroes are now serving them daily because of the application of the nonviolent, good will direct action technique. If the protesters are thrown out of a restaurant on their heads and sustain an injury, they do not go back to throw a brick in the window; they do not go back to shoot anybody; they do not go back to call anybody a bad name. We assume some suffering must be endured to break down these barriers. That is a part of the struggle. We carefully select the people who are to play their part in the application of this technique. They are rigidly disciplined. They must understand and know that not even a curse word is to be used against the person who attacks them violently or denies them the right of being served.

We have also applied this technique in Washington, which is practically the same as Georgia. We went into about fifteen different places, but we were not served. We finally left after remaining in these places some three or four hours. Of course, we will go back, and we will continue to go back until some change is brought about.

Nonviolent direct action is based on the theory of the organic unity of mankind. We believe that constantly conditioning people, by exposing them to the fact that the minorities are insisting upon their rights, will result in the eventual recognition of the soundness and necessity of abolishing discrimination.

I have practiced this myself. I went into the deep South some time ago, and went into the diner for the first time in my life. When I went toward the diner, the steward was coming out. Seeing that I was going toward the diner, he turned and went back. When I got to the door he pointed to a seat and I took it. Presently a white man came to the table and began talking to me. We talked about the war and the weather. Presently a Marine officer came, and we all sat and talked. This was so strange and so unusual that the waiter who was serving me evidently told all the kitchen crew that a colored man was in the diner, for each man of the kitchen crew came to the door and peeped at me.

The next day I went into the diner, and again I was served. One morning on my return trip, we were in the deep South, and we did not have a diner attached to the train. I went into the lounge car. There were eight white people there, two of them white women, and in the course of the conversation one of the women said, "We don't have a diner attached to the train, and we can't get anything to eat. But I have some apples and oranges, and I would like to share them with my neighbors." She got up and passed them around, and she asked if I would accept an orange. My first impulse was to refuse, but I decided I would accept and see what would happen. She gave me an apple and an orange, and we all sat and talked about the war. Presently she announced that she was from Culpepper, Virginia.

What does it prove? It proves that if you let the people alone, they will get along all right.

In conclusion, it appears to me that racial tension and racial riots will increase notably during the postwar period. I can see that reaction is on the march; reaction, not only against minorities, but against the very concept of democracy. It is obvious that we are going to have manifestations of racial violence in the various centers of this country unless measures are taken to prevent these outbursts. They are going to occur, because the Negroes are in motion. The minorities are in motion, and they are moving against the stereotypes, practices, and customs which hedge people in and deny them certain rights. It is utterly impossible for the minorities to stop moving against these barriers. Motion is inevitable. Motion is the law of their nature now; it is a law of progress.

Consequently, they are going to come into conflict with the fact of segregation and discrimination. The result will be social and racial explosions. But I consider that this is a healthful condition, despite the fact that we want to avoid violence. I consider it a condition of social pain that accompanies progress or out of which progress must come; it is impossible to avoid it. We may be able to assuage and ameliorate the pain by setting up commissions on race in the various parts of the country, but I expect to see Negroes driven off jobs by sheer physical violence. I expect to see anti-Semitism growing in this country everywhere.

Already in Boston, Providence, Pittsburgh, and New York, there are disgraceful manifestations of anti-Semitism among the people. I travel all over the country, and I have seen signs of increased opposition and antagonism to the Negro people, to the Mexicans, to the Jews, and to the Catholics.

In the southern section of this country, Catholics are hated. You recall that when Al Smith ran for the Presidency, five southern states broke away from the solid South because they spread the propaganda that, if Al Smith were elected, the Pope would sit in the White House. All over the South there is violent hatred of the Catholics.

There is also violent hatred of the Jews. I have had some interesting experiences traveling throughout the country. I have been in places where people have said, "I would rather sit by you than sit by that Jew." When they observed my reaction, there was a violent hatred in their faces against me. "Think of a Negro not wanting a white man to sit beside him," they grumbled to themselves.

So, unless there is unity on the part of labor, the Negro, and other minorities, a wave of reaction is going to arise in America. As I see it, there will be less democracy in this country than before the war began. It is evident today that democracy is in retreat in America. There is a tendency to move backwards. Also, in the international world there is that spirit of reaction.

As a matter of fact, all of us wanted the Axis powers to be destroyed, but the victory of the United Nations over the Axis powers has not meant the victory of democracy. We won the war in Burma, but we may lose it in Washington, D.C.

There are people in this country who would rather have seen the United States lose the war than see the Negroes receive their rights, or the Jews receive proper consideration, or the Catholics get justice. Therefore, today there is a great challenge to the people of liberal opinion and to labor to hold the line against reaction. Not only do we find that the retreat is on in various sections of the world, but the major revolutions of the past twenty-five years have been Bolshevist, Fascist, and Nazi, have been counter-democratic, and there is no indication that we can rally the peoples of the world around democratic slogans any more. Hence the outlook and the future of the world of labor and of the minorities is black, unless all minorities and the liberal and labor forces unite and fight for freedom, peace, and plenty, the international control of the atom bomb with international inspection of facilities for making atom bombs in all countries, world disarmament and democratic socialism.

VII

REMINISCENCES OF THE FAIR
EMPLOYMENT PRACTICE COMMITTEE

BY

MALCOLM ROSS

*Former Chairman, President's Committee on Fair Employment
Practice*

I should like to present some of the impressions, official and otherwise, which I picked up during the course of traveling around the
country on official business for the Fair Employment Practice Committee in 1944–45. I want to discuss three cities. The first of them is
San Antonio. It is a charming city, has good people. They are not
intolerant. They are the victims, as far as racial prejudice is concerned, of some old, deeprooted habits.

San Antonio has been Spanish longer than it has been American.
The Spaniards built fine old convents and cloisters. The five-foot
walls built by converted Indians still stand. The most famous of
course is the Mission of the Alamo.

The Battle of the Alamo, where more than one hundred men died
to a man, is considered an Anglo-Saxon bit of heroism. It is forgotten that among those who fell were Latin Americans. Old Davey
Crockett died within those walls, old Indian fighters, and professional
military men. With them died Latin Americans, who were also on
the side of freedom.

What happened to San Antonio in the course of the century since
the Alamo to make Mexican-Americans, some of them resident a
century longer in this country than the Anglo-Saxons who came
across the plains in the middle 1800's, the victims of race prejudice?

I think probably this prejudice has its roots in the economic situation. Contractors brought thousands and thousands of Mexican peons across the border because they were very cheap workers. You cannot have very low wage groups competing with higher wage groups on racial lines without having prejudice. Prejudice extends from the refusal of an opportunity to earn a living out into the other phases of life.

Until very recently, whole families of Mexican-Americans in San Antonio, including parents, children, aunts, and cousins, would have to work in order to make enough income for a family. Now one or two members of the family can earn as much as the whole family did before. The Wages and Hours law did that, and is a start toward better conditions.

One of the great airfields at San Antonio had the habit of keeping all Mexicans at common labor. The Anglo-Saxons had all the skilled jobs. Some of the workers complained to the Fair Employment Practice Committee. We went in. We presented the case to the Army authorities in charge. The Army was also bound by Executive Order not to discriminate. The Mexican-American boys were allowed their chance to use the skills which they had acquired and wanted to devote to the war effort; they were put to work at proper jobs.

Let me turn to New Orleans. The first day I was in New Orleans, having just left San Antonio, a great industrialist, a president of a railroad, gave an interview which was printed in the New Orleans papers. He said that New Orleans would have a thriving seaport for years to come because the trade with Latin America to the southward would keep the ships going.

I thought immediately of one fly in that ointment. New Orleans has few Mexican-Americans, but there are three millions of them westward in Texas, New Mexico, California, and Colorado. Whenever the Mexican-American citizen, no matter how many generations he has been here, is kept at the lowest wages in mining, and an Anglo-Saxon gets work doing the same thing at a salary that is much higher, word of it crosse the border down into Mexico. It does not help the Good Neighbor policy. The Port of New Orleans has a stake in the decent treatment of Mexican-Americans and the provision of fair opportunities in the rest of the country.

New Orleans, too, is a city that has been Spanish and French longer than it has been American. To be a Creole is a very proud thing in New Orleans. Various races have gone into the American bloodstream down there. The foreign races of New Orleans can no longer be distinguished. They are all very similar, except one minority, the 200,000 Negroes. They, as are Mexican-Americans, are identifiable. They remain open to any discrimination which anyone wishes to exercise against them.

In New Orleans, too, the root of the matter lies in the economic status. Once the Negro had a slave status, a cotton-chopping and a cotton-picking status, in all that territory. The habit of considering him as the man on the end of the pick, broom, or shovel is very strong and very old. It has kept a low wage group within the South.

New Orleans is a fine town. It is a tolerant town. For one thing, the Negroes there made the hand-wrought iron balconies that are like lace over New Orleans buildings. I think from that wrought-iron work grew the tradition of letting Negroes enter the building trades, so that many unions today are composed of Negro carpenters, masons, and bricklayers. New Orleans is far advanced over any other southern city in the degree to which Negroes are allowed in the building trades.

Nevertheless, the Negroes of New Orleans are a great problem in that city. I talked with some of the white lawyers and businessmen of the city. They are worried, and want to do things to give the Negro better opportunities. They are particularly worried about housing, and well they might be. There are Negroes living ten to a room, in terrible, bare, yellow buildings made of wood, extending a block deep, and no better than permanent barracks. In them people sleep in shifts. That, too, goes with low economic status, and so do badly paved streets, and no tax returns, and many other things.

As long as the South says that Negroes are a class apart and must stay at low wages, so long will the South remain industrially poor.

That is not to say that Negroes all expect to be elevated into skilled work. All they want is the opportunity if they have the skill. If the superior craftsmen among them acquire skills, then they want the chance to use their skills, and to become foremen if they are good enough.

Near New Orleans the Fair Employment Practice Committee had a case with a shipyard. That shipyard traditionally condemned all Negroes to common labor. The government during the war spent vast sums on training schools, and many Negroes went through those training schools at government expense. Then they found that the tradition of the community was against letting them be welders, chippers, and riveters. What happened? Trained Negroes went north, many of them, crowding northern cities, creating problems in northern cities. It will take a long while to readjust them in society.

It hurts a man, if he has gone through a training course and acquired skill, to be told that we need ships, that here is the way and there is the hull, but that the work is not for him.

This particular shipyard was so much in need of welders that it finally took the chance and hired Negro welders. The first ship which came off one of the ways where the work crews were Negroes broke a record in the yard for the building of a tanker. It was launched in sixty-one days. Is there more proof needed that Negroes can do good work, given the chance?

A common complaint is that the Negro will never have the skills the white man has. All generalities are dangerous. You cannot say that, because some Negroes will surprise you and come up with some amazing skills. It is true that the sons of field hands, with no education, have a tougher time on the way up than the sons of white mechanics who have played with monkey wrenches and bicycles and tools all their growing years. But the war proved, by and large, that the Negroes and the Mexican-Americans have inherent ability.

Let me take you to a town that I think will shock you. It shocked us of the Committee who sat there. Opposite St. Louis is the town of Alton, Illinois. Alton is the place where Lovejoy, the first newspaper martyr in this country, persisted in writing in his little sheet his disbelief in Negro slavery. A mob came and killed Lovejoy and threw his press in the river. That was one hundred years ago.

That countryside still suffers from the mob spirit. Alton has Negroes living there and working there. But three miles south, and hardly to be distinguished from it across an invisible town line, is East Alton. For fifty-two years, few Negroes have crossed the line of East Alton; if they have, they have seen the signs saying, "Don't let the sun set on you in East Alton."

No Negro except one man, an engineer who died twenty years ago, has ever worked in East Alton. The FEPC had a case there. It was the case of a munition firm whose plants all over the country made every third bullet fired by American guns during the war. In East Alton it had a plant employing ten thousand white workers, no Negroes. I asked the eighty-five year old native Vermonter who heads this great industry, how this started. Why is it that no Negroes can work in East Alton?

He told me that a couple of years before he went there in the early 1890's, the farmer who owned most of the countryside had difficulties with a Negro. There must have been serious difficulty, because a mob chased the Negro out into a cornfield and stayed there all night waiting to shoot him in the morning. He escaped during the night. But the memory of that incident lingered, grew up as a tradition of that place. When the powder mills started, no Negroes, except the one engineer, worked there. Now it had ten thousand people, brought in from all over the countryside to make the thing we needed most to win the war. No Negroes could go there.

In the first day of our hearing, there were three of us: a Negro member, Milton Webster, a woman member, Sarah Southall, and myself. They gave us for the hearing room the top of the town hall, with an American flag in back, a jail underneath. It was a typical, little, red brick town hall of a small town.

There was a local minister on the stand, testifying that none of his congregation of three hundred and sixty would permit Negroes to live or work in that town. He did not apologize for the fact; he just stated it on the witness stand under oath as a fact.

While he was so testifying, the brass mill boys went on a strike and came up to harass our meeting. The brass mill boys are rough and tough. They came with their hats on, cocky, and they marched down the aisle, and marched around our table and stood between us and the American flag. They blocked the windows and packed the hall sixteen deep. They were not there for the fun of it. One of them testified later, when we put him on the stand, that they had come over there to escort the Negro on my staff out of East Alton. They did not do it. But they did take the stand, one after the other, and testified that no Negro is ever going to work in that town.

The mayor of the town took the stand and gave the same testimony. A school teacher gave the same testimony, a little shame-facedly. Under questioning, he said that his great problem was not the kids in the schoolroom, but overcoming the home influence on those kids.

That is about as near as we got to any confession from the stand that life in East Alton was not all sweetness and light.

There was one man who looked, with his great eagle nose, fine blue eyes, and shock of white hair, like the substantial citizen of the town he was. He was the most vocal and bitter about his feeling that no Negroes were ever coming to that town. We questioned him. He said that the hand of government coming into that town to take away the rights of those local citizens was worse than the Ku Klux Klan.

We asked him, "What rights are we taking away from you?" It turned out he was talking about the rights of having restrictive covenants in the town, which we had no power to say anything about. He thought we were coming there to force them to sell their houses to Negroes. The fear of a possible loss of value was the great American right that he was standing on. It could not be talked out of him.

One of the ministers testified that his congregation would never allow any Negroes into East Alton. He came up to me later and he said, "You're doing a great work." I thought to myself that he might have said something of that kind on the witness stand. It would have been the one note in East Alton of that kind.

This is a sad story. What is the answer? Perhaps it goes back to the company, the church people, the officials of the town; they have not made a move in this realm for half a century. It goes back to the education of the kids of that town, to the prejudice handed down to them by their grandpappies.

We have to make a start on such prejudices somewhere, somehow. I suppose it is the duty of the more privileged men and women to make a start. We white collar people who live at one end of town in comfortable houses can think about these things, worry about them. But where prejudice has to be faced directly is at the work bench.

The employer who needs labor desperately may not mind whether the skills he needs come from a yellow, white, or black hand. But prejudice—that schism in the American soul between our professed democracy and our practice of it—may make his workers lay down their tools when minority group workers are brought into the plant.

Again, it may be that the employer is not wholly on the side of the angels. He may simply be offering the excuse that his workers will not work with Negroes, or with Mexican-Americans, or with Jews, or with Roman Catholics. We have called many of those bluffs. We have found that the exaggerated fears of employers turned out to be something very much less.

Nevertheless, it must be said in all honesty that this problem of curing the prejudice of workers at the roots is a tough one. This prejudice, too, I think stems from economic causes.

Most unions in this country were born in a time of economic scarcity. They went through various depressions when to have any work was income, and they protected income for the union members. They did not want to share that with outsiders. What is more understandable than not wanting to share it with someone of a different race, or manner of speech, or color, than oneself?

This instinct for self-protection is not confined to any type of organization or any race. There have always been minorities, and put-upon minorities, in this country.

The first of them were Irish Catholics. The Irish came over here during the potato famines, and, as the Mexican peons who crossed the line, worked for very low wages. The half-starved Irish immigrant was willing to work for one dollar a day on the railroads, to carry hods. The lucky Irishman got on the New York police force. He had his rough times, as you all well know. The Know-Nothing Party for ten years devoted its energies to anti-Catholic prejudice. The Ku Klux Klan, and its revival in our times, also started primarily with the idea of pushing down somebody for fear he might get one's job.

In the packinghouse industry, the Germans came over after the Irish had a start in the industry. The Irish, who had become Americans by that time, picked on the German element. But in time both the Germans and the Irish went to American schools and came out Americans, and with their full adoption into the national life, their racial antagonisms within the packinghouse industry disappeared. Let us now consider how this same sort of economic rivalry worked out within this industry for Negroes.

After World War I, employers rather generally said, "Let's be rid of this unionism that we have had to take during the war under government compulsion to accept collective bargaining." To do so, some of the packinghouse employers brought in Negroes as strike breakers. That was in 1919, when war jobs were over, when the guy on the street, white and colored, was worrying about what he was going to do. The Negroes took jobs in the packinghouses, and their loyalty went to the employer. He had rescued them from being on the street. The unions had done nothing to win the Negroes' loyalty to them.

So the white strikers stayed out on the street, the Negro stayed inside. And all during the 1920's animosity, made deep by what had happened, continued between the whites and the blacks in that industry.

Then when the industry was organized in the 1930's, the union had the good sense to see that, if you leave any divisive minority off by itself, it is a temptation for the employer to keep the union weak, to lower wages, to break strikes. Not all employers have those desires, but many have in the past, and some may again. The packinghouse workers, and many other unions, refused to let the color line divide them. Today they have a completely integrated union, in which nobody can set off one racial group as a means of creating internal dissension.

Do they have trouble still? Plenty of it. Wild-cat strikes still happen because of racial prejudice. Whole locals are infected, so that the top union command worries whether it can keep control of them. People inside sometimes use the color line to divide the membership for their own purposes. It is tough to keep discipline in these unions. But the ones who are doing that tough job know that their work has strengthened the unions.

In 1942, there was a handful, comparatively speaking, of Negroes and Mexican-Americans in war industries. In 1944, there were probably a million and a half Negroes in all war industries, and certainly some 800,000 in the prime war industries which reported to the War Manpower Commission. They were mostly newcomers. Of course, when cutbacks came in shipping, aircraft, ammunition, and metal industries, they were among the first to go. That was not unfair. The seniority rule should not be tampered with.

I think it is a good thing that the State of New York in 1944 said there will be no discrimination in this state because of race, creed, or color or national origin. It is a good thing for business, for trade unions, for moral force, that the State of New York had made the decision that the opportunities of peacetime employment are going to be offered equally to all its citizens.

There are plenty of safeguards against unjust decisions. In the case of the New York State law, state budget officers will want to know whether the commission is misusing its authority. The Legislature will scan it carefully. The public will. The man who thinks he is hurt by it can protest loudly. There is sufficient recourse against unfair treatment.

The FEPC received four thousand cases in 1944. We dismissed two thirds of them. In that respect we were a safety valve for people who thought they had cause to complain of discrimination. If they did not have, we did not take the case. We settled more than one thousand cases in which we found valid evidence of discrimination.

VIII

LABOR AND THE INTERNATIONAL
LABOR ORGANIZATION

BY

CARTER GOODRICH

*Professor of Economics, Columbia University; Former Chairman,
Governing Body, International Labor Office*

What of labor's participation in the carrying out of a program of
international reconstruction? Here part of the answer lies with the
International Labor Organization. The ILO provides a direct channel for the participation of labor in official international decisions.
This was a great innovation made at the Paris Peace Conference of
1919. The constitution of the ILO as drawn up at that time introduced into international organization a wholly new principle. The
organization is fully official. Its members are nations. Its only source
of financial support is from government appropriations. The innovation was this, that in such an official organization, in all of its
councils, representatives of employers and of workers take part on
equal terms with the representatives of governments.

In the governing body of the International Labor Office, there are
sixteen government seats, eight workers' seats and eight employers'
seats. To the International Labor Conference each member nation is
entitled to send two government delegates, one workers' delegate and
one employers' delegate, with various technical advisers. In each case
the worker or employer is entirely free to speak and vote on the opposite side of a question from the representative of his own government, and very often does so.

According to the constitutional provision which governs the choice
of these delegates, the members—these you will recall are the gov-

ernments—undertake to nominate nongovernment advisers chosen in agreement with the industrial organizations, if such organizations exist, which are most representative of employers or workers as the case may be in their respective countries.

This element of tripartite structure is of the first importance. The ILO is not, as some people assume from its name, a labor organization or a federation of unions. Labor's voting strength inside the ILO is twenty-five per cent, not one hundred per cent, and it is exactly equal to that of industry. Therefore, it goes without saying that the ILO is not a substitute for labor's own organizations either national or international, but the significant fact is that the ILO is an agency in which the representatives of workers and employers alike can collaborate officially and effectively with the representatives of governments. From this has come the realism, the vigor, much of the saltiness of ILO discussions and debates. In this fact lies the explanation for its survival and much of the promise for its future.

But what has the ILO done? What is the organization for? The preamble to the constitution starts with a very magnificent general statement, the statement that universal peace can be established only if it is based upon social justice. To that it adds a more specific note of explanation. It says: "Conditions of labor exist involving such injustice, hardship, and privation to large numbers of people as to produce unrest so great that the peace and harmony of the world is in peril."

The organization's function is international action for the removal of such conditions. Its principal although not its sole method has been the formulation of international minimum standards of labor conditions, taking the form of conventions or labor treaties intended for ratification and application by national action. These standards are the product of tripartite discussions in the annual International Labor Conferences. There they are fought over and argued out clause by clause and line by line in the give and take of a sort of international collective bargaining carried on by representatives of governments, employers, and workers from many countries. Then, after that process, they are taken back to the individual countries for consideration by the national authorities, and they re-

ceive the binding force of law when and only when they are ratified
by the individual nations. In all, sixty-seven such labor conventions
or treaties were adopted up to 1944, and eight hundred and eighty-
seven national acts of ratification. In addition, the conferences had
adopted about the same number of recommendations, which do not
take the form of treaties but which often have had equally important
influence on national policy.

These conventions have covered a wide variety of labor and social
conditions.

None has so far attempted to set rates of wages internationally.
On the other hand, treaties dealing with the hours of labor have had
widespread influence and so, also, have the standards adopted for social insurance, a field in which the ILO did a good deal of pioneering. Other conventions deal with employment, protection against
disease and accident, and the prohibition of child labor. Two subjects particularly appropriate to the International Labor Organization
have been the protection of migrants working in countries other
than their own and the protection of labor in colonial or dependent
territories.

In the case of shipping, the most international of all industries, a
particularly extensive body of regulations has been worked out in
a series of special conferences, of which the ship owners and seamen
are so proud that they lump all the work of the ILO into the Maritime
Conventions and the Land Conventions. As one example of the seamen's code, we have the right of the seaman to his wages after his
ship has been wrecked.   .

This developing of the international labor code has been and remains partial and uneven in the coverage of subject matter, in its
degree of acceptance, and in the strictness of its enforcement. It has
been a beginning, not a completed achievement, but even so it represents a substantial body of accepted obligations already in force
and the marshaling of world opinion for the extension of international standards not yet everywhere attained.

In the meanwhile, the International Labor Office, the permanent
secretariat and staff of the organization, with headquarters in Geneva,
with a farflung network of branches and correspondents throughout

the world, had become a great center of information on labor legislation and labor problems. In the summer of 1940 its working center
was moved to Montreal. Its influence is exerted partly through its
publications and partly by means of missions in which experts from
the permanent staff visit particular nations at the request of their
governments to give advice on matters of labor administration.

The annual conferences, moreover, have provided an international
talking place in which representatives of governments, employers,
and workers from all over the world have debated questions of social
policy. Each year the range of these discussions has been far wider
than the subject matter of any specific conventions or recommendations that were on the agenda of the conference. In recent years these
discussions have shown a deepening realization of the fact that the
raising of labor and living standards depends fundamentally upon
the development of a sound and expanding economy.

It may be appropriate to add, as the book goes to press (February,
1947), a brief comment on the active postwar program of the International Labor Office. International Labor Conferences were held at
Philadelphia in 1944, at Paris in 1945, and at Seattle and at Montreal
in 1946. Of these the Seattle meeting was devoted to the problems of
seamen. The total number of conventions is now 80 and there have
been 927 national acts of ratification. One of the Seattle conventions
has for the first time set an international minimum wage standard—
for A B's in the merchant marine. The 1947 Conference will meet
in Geneva in June. Innovations since the war are the creation of Industry Committees in seven great world industries and the decision
to hold an Asiatic Regional Conference.

On December 14, 1946, the General Assembly of the United Nations ratified an agreement reached between the two organizations
by which the International Labor Office, retaining its autonomy and
its tripartite structure, is recognized as one of the specialized agencies
of the United Nations. Thus the work of the International Labor
Office becomes an integral part of the great enterprise of the United
Nations and its associated institutions.

II. LABOR AND THE CHURCH

IX

LABOR'S CHALLENGE TO THE CHURCH

BY

KERMIT EBY

Director of Education and Research, Congress of Industrial Organizations

Two developments in modern Protestantism have been discussed and written about frequently. They are: (1) the tendency of the established denominations, Presbyterians, Methodists, Baptists, etc., to become more middle class and "respectable"; (2) the tendency on the part of workers to stay away from religious services in greater and greater numbers, or, if they do go to church, to attend one of the rapidly growing cults.

It is my intention to discuss these trends and conclude with some practical suggestions which might be helpful in reversing them. The observations and suggestions which I shall make will be deeply colored by personal experience and reaction.

My family were members of the Church of the Brethren (Dunkers). For my first sixteen years I missed church only one time, and that was because of measles. During each winter we had revival meetings lasting from two to four weeks. Sin was real in our little Dunker community and souls were in need of saving. Sinners included drinkers of hard cider, gamblers at cards, fornicators and adulterers, buyers on charge accounts, and Socialists. Sin was a personal, not a social matter at Baugo church, and we believed the sinner capable of repenting and building a new life.

The souls of all the sinners were declared to be of equal value in the sight of God, and yet each winter when the revival-meeting minister and our church's presiding elders called on the unsaved, I remember they spent much more time on the owners of farms and the payers of cash than they did on the improvident and unsuccessful. A farm owner with money in the bank commanded more attention than the unmarried mother of a nameless child.

At Baugo, as in thousands of other country, town, or city churches, we worshipped the goddess Success. Farms and bank accounts, business and profits, were the criteria by which we really lived, and, to a large extent, are still the standards by which we live. To this day my most marked feeling of inferiority grows out of the fact that I have no farm paid for, no sense of economic security.

However, to be perfectly fair, we were not without a sense of responsibility for our fellow men. We supported missions, concerned ourselves with the plight of our colored brethren across the seas— and were comparatively blind to the evils around us at Baugo. And in so doing, we were not different from our Protestant brethren in thousands of other Baugos.

Time brought changes. The sons and daughters of Baugo could not all be absorbed into our rural life. We moved to the city, worked hard, saved our money, got ahead because of disciplined attitudes and habits, moved to good residential districts, and built ourselves a nicely restricted little Protestant haven. Our church, like our club, could be attended only by those who could afford it, who had the money to buy good clothes, and who could keep up their contributions.

As these trends progressed and Protestantism moved out of town to the suburbs, America was rapidly changing from an agricultural to an industrial society. More and more persons were becoming dependent upon wages for a livelihood, fewer and fewer were capable of lifting themselves from the class into which they were born. The attainment of security and freedom from want was no longer possible solely through individual effort.

These developments are well known. There is no need to describe them further. Instead, I wish to stress the steps which led to my present conviction that organized religion must concern itself more and more with the problems of the underprivileged.

My Sunday school teacher taught me that Jesus was concerned with the poor and oppressed. He identified Himself, was one, with the hungry, the naked, and the sick. Later I learned it was the poor who first accepted His teachings *en masse*. And still later I learned that we respectable Methodists, Presbyterians, and Baptists are the children of the underprivileged poor and those who toil.

Today, while many of my attitudes have changed, there is no escaping the conviction of my responsibility to help those who are less fortunate. I am active in the labor movement less by choice than by accident. Actually, if the church was as militant for the values which concern me most, I would be working in it instead of in the CIO. Probably when the labor movement becomes respectable, radicals like myself will once more find a haven in the church. I devoutly hope so.

That hope grows out of the conviction that man does not live by bread alone, even though I recognize the importance of bread. It grows out of my belief that a materialistic interpretation of history is not enough, out of a belief that people are important and that each person counts. Men are not created to be the pawns of their more ambitious fellow men.

Organized religion, then, if it is to save itself, must become more closely identified with the everyday aspirations of people. The church must be at least as human as labor, its leaders more sensitive to mankind's struggle, if it is to regain the ground lost in recent years. Those who would bring religion to the people must live with the people. Sermons and exhortations will not do the job. The confidence of the worker can be won only by those who are willing to preach less and live more. We must get over our concept of doing things *for* people, and work *with* them. Christmas baskets and philanthropy are mockeries in an economy in which poverty is an anachronism.

It seems to me the labor movement is more sensitive to this fact than is any other part of our society. We believe that hunger in the midst of plenty is sin, and that the creation of artificial scarcities to keep up prices so that profits can be maintained, is the essence of evil. Putting it bluntly, labor is determined no longer to be tolerant of an economic system in which one third of the people are ill clothed, ill housed, and underfed. The workers believe the common man is coming into his own.

It was this feeling of identification with the peoples of the world which stimulated labor's all-out war effort. The war in which we engaged was a part of a world movement against fascism and reaction, against the destruction of democracy, free trade unions, and civil and religious liberty.

The possibility of the betrayal of this movement and of the triumph of reaction here in the United States is becoming ever more a concern of the leaders of labor. That is the reason for the beginning of political action by labor. Leaders of organized labor feel themselves more and more isolated, and more and more convinced that their unions must not be destroyed. They believe, and so do I, that we must have a strong and militant trade union movement for economic democracy here at home.

During the war everyone had a job. If there is any one conviction most stubbornly shared by workers, it is that they will not go back to breadlines. Full employment for everyone willing to work, is the aim of the workers of America; learning to live with plenty, the task of the twentieth century. In the words of Howard Vincent O'Brien, "If we can produce enough gun carriages, we can produce enough baby carriages!"

If you and I are to serve our generation well, we must be capable of great indignation and never silent in the presence of sin. There is no greater evil than hunger in the midst of plenty. A society which can produce guns, planes, and ships, must produce houses, schools, and playgrounds for happy families and healthy children. Those who stand in the way of such an achievement are sinners, and it is our task to convict them of their sin. A militant effort to bring about the age of the common man and the elimination of poverty is the alternative to wars and revolution.

Next to the elimination of the sin of poverty, those who lead labor, particularly in the CIO, are sensitive to the dangers of racial and religious antagonisms. Organized labor cannot exist if anti-Semitism is not wiped out, the Negro lifted to complete equality, and Catholicism accepted along with Protestantism. Here is another front on which the church and labor must fight together; for if reaction triumphs, anti-Semitism mounts, race riots flare up, religious tensions mount, and labor is strait-jacketed and crushed, the days of the church will be numbered. Pastor Niemöller is reported to have said to his fellow ministers as he was marched off to a concentration camp, "If you would guard your own liberty, protect the liberty of the first minority attacked!" There are no inferiors among those created in the image of God.

Prophecy is not my gift. However, one does not need to be a prophet to risk saying that the days of white supremacy and imperialism are dead and that the nation or race which attempts to impose its will on the colored peoples of the world is inviting wars and suffering.

Those of us interested in preventing such a catastrophe can begin at home. The American Negro must be given full citizenship. The discrimination he suffers cannot be tolerated indefinitely. Either we make this democracy of ours work, or it will die.

If men are good enough to work together under union contracts, they are good enough to worship together, to study together, and to live in the same neighborhoods.

Perhaps the idea I am trying to convey can be most clearly expressed as follows: the abstract concepts of justice, brotherhood, liberty, equality, and fraternity must be given specific meaning. It is not enough to be in favor of justice; we must translate our ideas into jobs and houses, schools, and equal educational and job opportunity for black and white.

The path to hell is paved with good intentions. There are no half-way measures in times like these. Although there have been times when, because of beliefs like these, I have been called "communist," at no time have I been tempted to join that fundamentalist sect. Nevertheless, in some ways Russia offers the world a great challenge. There is much sympathy for the concrete achievements of Russia in the ranks of organized labor. This sympathy grows out of a profound respect for Russian resistance to fascist aggression; but it is also affected by Russian mastery of Western technology and its use for social ends, and by Russian acceptance of race equality. Russia may not have the political democracy we boast of; but she may have some of the security we, because of our great wealth, could easily attain.

Those who have studied mankind say his goals throughout the millennia have been freedom and security. I have no quarrel with this interpretation. I wish to emphasize the trite observation that security without freedom is slavery; and freedom without security, intolerable.

We in America have suffered much from insecurity in recent years, and made much of liberty. Not so long ago, millions were unemployed; breadlines were everywhere. While there is now full employment, millions believe this condition cannot last. Because of the war, tremendous shifts have taken place in our civilian population. Millions of persons moved from south to north in quest of jobs. Face to face with the problems of our industrial society for the first time, most have brought with them their prejudices, their religious and racial bigotry, their fundamentalist theology, and their religious otherworldliness. Detroit has over two thousand hillbilly preachers. Gerald P. Smith and Frank Norris are their models, hatred their incentive.

Many of these ministers are subsidized by wealthy reactionaries. Churches are built and financed for them. Those who would bring Fascism to America seek to do so by building on this indigenous foundation of Ku Klux Klanism. Unless we open our churches and learn to lead where these others betray, reaction will triumph in Detroit and spread from city to city.

A religion of intolerance is dangerous to our life and our institutions and smacks of the Nazis. Decrying those who are attracted by its inflammatory qualities will not solve the problem. As I see it, there is only one solution: the development of a society made up of mentally healthy people. That is no easy task. It will take the combined efforts of all men of good will. Included in the program must be, not only plans for job security, but provisions for healthy recreational outlets, for group play and community life. Peoples of different social and religious backgrounds must be brought together, learn to know each other. Then there must also be provisions for adequate housing, social security, and, above all, educational opportunities.

We must educate first. Every technique known to man must be used to combat racism and intolerance; movies, comic strips, radio are our tools. We must enlist them to overcome the rantings of the bigoted.

For years I have dreamed of the church militant, dreamed of the time when the best of our youth would be equipped to go into these areas of social tension and work together with the people in the achievement of brotherhood. Is there any reason why this dream must be forever unrealized? Are we going on training our young men to fit themselves for middle-class pulpits in middle-class communities, ultimately to stagnate mentally and spiritually? We need some pioneers, men and women, who will strike out on new paths, men who are willing to break with their institutions and seek their compensations from their identification with the struggles of their fellow men.

In practically every paragraph I have stressed the integration of religion with life, the translation of the abstract into the specific, and the necessity for the yeast of Christian idealism to leaven the whole loaf of life. I have done so because I am convinced that a religion which is limited to ritual and attendance at church on Sunday is no religion at all. Our living today is not compartmentalized. Pious prayers are no help to exploited workers and ill fed, ill clad children.

Every time I hear someone quote, "The poor ye have always with you," I am tempted to do violence. People do not prefer poverty to jobs and clean homes.

Religion must be a part of life. Every act of ours must be influenced by a desire to make goodness attractive and the good life for all attainable.

Religion must not be an escape, but a challenge. Ours is the task of producing an environment which will produce a healthy people;

the task, in the words of Hermann Rauschning, of making the positive values of love and tolerance as dynamic as Hitler made hate and intolerance.

May I repeat, this is no easy task, and the times are dark and beset with wars and suffering.

Man's idealism, it seems to me, springs from his belief, and his belief, to have meaning, must find expression in action if it is not to die. A few days ago, I was discussing with a friend this fact as it applied to our church. We were impressed by the fact that, while our church is pacifist and we teach a pacifist doctrine, ninety-two per cent of our young people went into the Army, eight per cent into Conscientious Objector camps. After a long discussion, we agreed this was so because we had given our young people a revolutionary faith and no revolutionary program to match it.

Those interested in aiming at a program such as I have outlined must work toward: (1) placing human rights ahead of property rights; (2) recognizing at all times the dignity of man; (3) guaranteeing a job at a living wage for everyone willing and able to work; (4) achieving fair status for all members of minority groups; (5) developing labor-management cooperation; (6) eliminating poverty; (7) production for use, not profit; and (8) the development of education and of the healthy use of leisure time.

Throughout the past fifteen years, I have met many men, some who have received publicity and some who have not. Recently I have learned to know two men high in the ranks of labor, both of whom grew up as miners. Both have served the labor movement for years. The one is as good a man as I have ever met; the other, some say, in his ruthless drive for power is a devil. Many times I have asked myself, "Why the contrast?"

The only answer which suffices is that one is motivated by a belief that man has a soul and that mankind is sacred, while the other is basically contemptuous of his fellow men. The former sought power *with*, the latter power *over*.

If this sick civilization is to be healed, I will place my bet on the men who are not afraid to fail, but who strike out in new directions in the effort to save the world.

X

RELIGION'S CONTRIBUTIONS TO
LABOR LEADERSHIP

BY

BERNARD C. CLAUSEN

Minister, Euclid Avenue Baptist Church, Cleveland, Ohio

This is one of the tightest periods in human history. What intelligent churchmen and devoted labor leadership need now is the realization that it may not be as bad as it looks, and that, anyway, all of us need to keep a certain poise in the midst of it.

Unless I am mistaken, religion's part in labor's search for new horizons at this juncture is the production of that poise, that steady, patient, persistent, courageous inner attitude, that can confront the varying circumstances of labor's experience. I call it, for lack of a better name, "adult discount."

You know what happens to a young child in the movies. Psychologists say it is often a dreadful experience. They say: never take a little child to the movies unless you are sure what the story is going to be about and how it is to be treated. You may leave scars that will last for years.

Sooner or later these little children grow up, and as they grow up they achieve what most adults have achieved: the ability to sit through a movie without being seriously harmed by it.

There are three steps. First, the little child learns that everything going on around him is not necessarily happening to him. These emotional betrayals, these surgical operations, these shots in the dark, all seem to be aimed at the little child. Soon he discovers he can sit in the midst of them, surrounded by these sights and sounds, informed, influenced, but unharmed, behind a kind of barrier for his own protection.

99

Second, the little child learns that, when things happen to people, even in the movies, what is important is not what the things are doing to the people, but what the people are doing to the things. The child soon learns that people can be identified by causes, by ideals. Then, the more opposition, the more likely the life is to be significant. The measure of progress can be indicated largely by the drag back against the life that is making the progress. The child soon learns to honor his heroes by the enemies they make.

The third step is taken when the child learns that everything is coming out all right in the end. It does not often look that way. The more trouble, the merrier. The more trouble, the more likely that the situation is really significant.

Once the child has taken those three steps, the psychologists say the child has "adult discount" and never again will be seriously harmed by the movies, never again will be afraid or disturbed. He does not have to make up his mind or summon up his courage. He is equipped.

Churchmen and labor leaders alike need adult discount toward life. They achieve it by the same three steps. For these, religion as an institution can be responsible.

First, you must realize that not everything going on around you is necessarily happening to you. Relax, drop off care like a garment.

I am a Christian minister; I draw my illustrations from Jesus. You remember that story of Jesus in the storm on the little lake. The disciples were striving furiously to reach the shore before the boat was swamped. One of them caught sight of Jesus fast asleep on the stern seat. Angrily he cried, "Master, carest Thou not that we perish?" Instantly, Jesus was awake, ready to direct their efforts with fresh skill. When they wrote about it afterwards, they said it seemed that even the wind and the waves obeyed him. He had that marvelous poise to rest like a little child until he was needed, and then to concentrate his power on the immediate situation.

There is a second thing religion can provide for labor. It is the knowledge that when things happen to us, the important matter is not what the things do to us, but what we can do to the things.

Our significance is measured largely in terms of our opposition. Labor leaders need to know that.

I lived through the First World War. People sometimes said to me, "Aren't you afraid of war?" I hope I was not afraid of what it could do to me. But I was a little afraid of what I might not be able to do to war. I killed men then; there is blood on my hands. I came away from that horrible experience determined I would give my life to help prevent another war from breaking over young men. I did my best. You did your best. We did not do enough. But the moment you begin to get concerned about responsibilities like that, you are absorbed in what you can do to war, and have lost all fear of what injustice and misunderstanding and war can do to you.

Clifford Beers succumbed to mental collapse. Sent to an asylum, he came out, after many months, cured, not by the treatment but in spite of it. He was tempted to do what everybody else had done: try to forget it, never mention it. Someone whispered to him that what the insane people of America needed was a friend. Clifford Beers said, "By the grace of God I will be that friend. I will remember everything they did to me so that no one will ever have to suffer that kind of treatment again." By twenty-five years of ceaseless toil in the Mental Hygiene Association of America and the world, by single-handed, diligent, ceaseless efforts, he changed the whole attitude of humanity toward men and women in mental illness.

That is what labor leadership needs to get from the church: a profound and creative determination against being changed by things which oppose us. We must change the things.

The third thing all of us need to learn is that everything is going to come out all right in the end. There is no deeper confidence in religion than the understanding that God is not mocked. We are all impatient. We want life to be synchronized to the little tick-tick of our tiny cuckoo clocks, instead of the patient pendulum of God's purpose. Theodore Parker used to say, "I am always in a hurry. God never is." But God is getting somewhere.

The problem is how the institutions of religion are going to transmit that adult discount to labor leaders. You cannot shout it, you cannot write it, you cannot proclaim it, you cannot debate it. You must produce it. You must exemplify it. Again and again, against the local demands of the local situation you must fling the force of your faith into helpful and creative efforts with others. Do the best you can, and then relax and start all over again.

We had an interesting experience in Pittsburgh with a program of this kind. The problem there was incipient violence, as the unions began to be organized, against the grim disposition to fight them back on the part of the steel industry. Employers were determined the union should not get a chance. All the sociologists and economists in the country said, "Pittsburgh is the place where the big explosion is going to take place."

Pittsburgh passed through those years of critical pioneering for labor unions with no outburst of labor violence. I do not say the churches were responsible. I do say experiments were carried on there in terms of workers' education. Schools were established up and down the river valleys under the auspices of religious enthusiasts: not proclaiming, not arguing, not insisting, not evangelizing, not counting statistics, but putting the resources of decent social organization at the disposal of prospective labor union leaders. We used all the techniques of the Fabian socialists in England, which put its labor program a half-century ahead of America.

The result was, when the unions began to be formed, we had hundreds of young people in the towns up and down those rivers who knew sociology and economics and labor union history and public speaking and the art of democratic group life. They were committed to one thing: pride in peaceful negotiation rather than violence.

Even the industrialists are beginning to acknowledge the value of worker education. If they are going to be compelled to handle organized groups, the more the workers know about the problem, the better off all the factors are.

I cite that as an instance of a way to handle this tragic misunderstanding between religion and labor: not by hurried demands for attention, but by genuine cooperation at the level of local problems.

If by such comradeship, by the demonstration of these virtues in action, we are able to present a way of life that will give poise to labor leadership and to labor's ranks during the twisting torments of the days that are just ahead, then religious faith will have borne its share in exploring labor's new horizons, and then our theory will have had justification in practice.

XI

THE RECONCILIATION OF RELIGION AND LABOR

BY

JOHN G. RAMSAY

Public Relations Representative, United Steelworkers of America

I should like to begin by relating some of my earlier experiences as a steelworker. After spending seventeen years in the steel mills, I became a public relations representative of a great union, devoting the major part of my time to bridging the gaps between religion and labor.

When I first began working with unions, I was asked to leave the church. I did not leave it. When I was asked to leave, I raised the question, "Whose church is this?" I was asked what I meant. I said, "Well, if it belongs to the boss, I won't embarrass him any more, but if it belongs to Jesus Christ, I am going to stick." And so I stuck.

I think I am able to do the job I am doing today because of this experience in the church. Many of the boys in the labor movement who have had similar experiences left the church. I do not feel that they lost their religion. The labor movement became the outlet for that religious zeal. To me, those men who have built the great labor unions in our country have been motivated by a spiritual zeal which has made the labor unions do the kind of job they have done in raising and maintaining standards of living and working conditions.

My first experience in organizing was not in labor; it was with the Boy Scouts, Christian Endeavor, and Parent-Teacher Association. However, along in 1930 things were changed. The workers in the mills found themselves without jobs through no fault of their own. Since that time, I have realized that we ourselves were a great deal at fault, because we had not organized to take responsibility, and therefore we did not have a voice of any strength in the nation.

I helped the people who were unemployed to organize, so that they could have a united voice in bringing about the necessary changes to better the living conditions of their families. It was that experience that taught me to understand the objectives of the organized labor movement. A minister helped me a great deal to see that I must help with the problems of these people. This minister helped the people, he inspired them to organize to help themselves, he gave them courage, but eventually he paid the price by losing his church. The majority of his congregation were self-righteous, complacent, or controlled, and requested his resignation.

In working with the unemployed, I learned that the church had been sleeping on the job. The leadership that was offered to the unemployed, when they developed a state and national organization, was not a leadership that came from the church. The radical ideologists had had foresight, and had trained leadership for these times, but the churches had failed to have that vision, and their people were not prepared. That is why I was not understood in my own church. The church had failed to educate the membership of its congregations on the social pronouncements of religion.

In those days, I made statements concerning the things I felt and saw that were considered very radical. I did not realize that the church had made those statements long ago. If I had known, and had been able to quote the pronouncements of the church, it would have been much easier for me. I do urge the religious leaders in our nation to see that their people know the social promulgations of their religion.

We find all the different religions have a social vision. The religious groups, Catholic, Protestant, and Jewish, have upheld the right of labor to organize. Most of the workers did not know this until, in an organizing campaign, the labor leaders publicized it. My union, the United Steelworkers, CIO, published a leaflet, *The Church Speaks Out for Labor*. In it, we quoted from the various religious faiths about labor's right to organize. Many of us learned for the first time that long before there was a national law upholding labor's right to organize, religion had stood by that belief.

My first experience organizing outside of the mills was in Buffalo, New York. I want to tell you some of the experiences I had there, so that you can understand some of the trouble that organized labor has had with the churches. I was called to Buffalo, not to get men to join the union, but because in a few of the churches ministers and priests were preaching against the union from their pulpits. I was tremendously helped by Reverend James Myers, who had previously invited me to serve on the Industrial Division of the Federal Council of the Churches of Christ in America. That was one thing that gave me an opening when I went into Buffalo. The first thing I did was to become acquainted with the secretary of the Council of Churches. I found him to be very cooperative.

Then I went to a labor union meeting to speak to the workers. I told them that the reason some of the ministers were preaching against the union was because they believed what had been told them by people who were not friendly to us, and that if our members had been wearing their union buttons to church and letting the people of the church and their minister know that they were in the union, they could have done a public relations job which only they could really do.

However, I asked them, if they had any particular problems, to bring them to me because I wanted to understand what they were. After that meeting, I heard a lot of stories. One of the men who came to me was very bitter, but I will tell of him because I want to show the extremes. I have told of a minister who lost his church because he spoke out for labor, but this worker's minister was preaching from his pulpit against labor. I called this minister on the telephone, and told him I was connected with the steelworkers' union and would appreciate an opportunity to tell him our side of the story. He told me it would not do any good, that his mind was made up, that we were a bunch of Communists, and that he was preaching against us.

I said, "Well, I will try another approach. I am a member of the Industrial Division of the Federal Council of Churches." He said,

"That doesn't help you a bit. That group is a disgrace to the country and ought to go to Russia."

I said, "Well, you sound rather impossible, but I understand now why one of your parishioners asked me to get in touch with you."

He asked me who it was and I told him. He said, "Why, he is a very fine man."

I said, "We also think he is; he is a potential leader in this union that we are building here. I want you to think about this tonight. Are you going to be responsible for giving to organized labor another bitter labor leader?" I added, "I hope your conscience bothers you, sir, and that you will call me back." This ended our conversation. Two days later I received a call from this minister, saying he would like to see me. Some families had left his church, and he realized it was because of his anti-union sermons. We got those families back into the church again.

We learned that the National Association of Manufacturers had given a dinner for the Buffalo clergymen. We do not object to that at all. It is their privilege. However, they had done a very good selling job to some of the clergymen. The NAM did not speak against the union, I understand; they just sold themselves as being good men.

At this time, in the newspapers of Buffalo there appeared some full-page advertisements. The following one, in the *Lackawanna Leader,* was supposed to be sponsored by working men, but those responsible were never identified:

A message to our fellow employees: At a time when our national defense is in jeopardy, this Committee comes to you with a sincere plea that you examine closely the aims, methods and possible results of our becoming organized under the banner of the CIO. Our American way of life will be no more, and we will face slavery under a ruthless master. Steel is a most important single item in our defense program. Without steel our fight for adequate national armament is lost. It does not greatly matter whether the master is Communist or Fascist, he is still utterly ruthless. Scores of honest and responsible persons throughout the country have charged the CIO with being dominated by Communists and the Communist party. The CIO and its officials have been unable honestly or successfully to deny these charges. It is so Communist-dominated and many other men working among us as organizers, both official and non-official, are Communists or Communist sympathizers. They seek to change our American way of life to the Communist way.

We are the last stronghold of democracy. It is in our hands that the future of our nation lies. It is in our hands that the future of the nation that guards us and gives us freedom and life lies. These charges have not been made carelessly. They are facts and have been presented with documentary and sworn testimony.

This advertisement was signed by a Fair Elections Committee. No one knew what the Fair Elections Committee was. We never had any open opposition to debate the issues before us in that election.

This was the reason why some of the clergy were preaching against the union. They had met some nice members of management at a dinner and then they read these false advertisements, accepting them without thinking too deeply about them.

The union leaders decided that if the National Association of Manufacturers could entertain at a dinner, we could afford to entertain at luncheon. So we invited the clergymen to have luncheon with us. We did not find that there was a sufficiently close relationship between the religious faiths to enable us to have them together. At one luncheon, we entertained the Protestant clergy and the Jewish rabbis. At another luncheon, we entertained the Catholic priests and the Negro clergy.

At the first luncheon, I introduced four local workers who had come to me with their problems with their churches, to tell the clergymen why they had joined the union. I wish I could give the exact speeches of those men. Each one was a story in itself, and their stories told what had made them union men. I do want to give the story of a Jewish worker, whom I introduced last. He had a wonderful personality. He said, "I didn't join the union to better myself in a material sense. I was the best pussyfooter in my department, and I got along with the boss, but," he said, "every man wanted to do what I was doing, and so we were jealous of each other. I began to see a change coming into the department, the men began to work together, and I investigated and found that they were joining the CIO. I also joined, wondering if they would take a Jew into that kind of brotherhood. They did, and as a result, this Catholic, this Protestant, and this Negro are buddies to a Jew."

One of the ministers remarked that this was a real sermon, and that it seemed this union, which some of them had preached against, was doing the things about which they had preached.

In arranging for the second luncheon, we went to see Bishop Duffy, and had a very frank talk with him. He gave us a letter to Mr. Vincent Sweeney, publicity representative of the Steel Workers Organizing Committee, in which he said:

Dear Mr. Sweeney:

The principle of unionism, after a long struggle, is recognized today by American citizens generally. It is worthwhile remembering, now that the idea of the union of the workers is an achieved conclusion, that the Catholic Church should be the defender of the inalienable right of labor to organize for collective bargaining in a day when such defense involves courage to support the principle. Not only the Bishops and priests of the Catholic Church, but the Popes, in a long series of encyclicals, emphasized that the workingman has the right and the duty to unionize in order to promote his own interests and to provide for the decent upbringing of his family.

The Catholic Church of the diocese of Buffalo has maintained this principle and will support it as the right of free men in the face of any difficulty.

With every good wish, I am,

Very sincerely yours, John A. Duffy, Bishop of Buffalo.

He allowed us to put that letter in the newspapers, and to put it in a pamphlet to pass out at the gates. He set aside a Sunday before our election for the Catholic priests to preach upon the Pope's encyclicals upholding labor's right to organize into unions for collective bargaining.

Then we had our luncheon with the Catholic priests, and invited the Negro ministers in with us. There was one priest in Buffalo, Father Charles Maxwell, who knew the workers, who had a heart for them. When the union had a strike in Lackawanna, he was out on the picket line upholding the rights of the workers, but telling them the right way to conduct themselves. There was no strife at the gates, until, one night, Father Maxwell became very tired. At two o'clock in the morning, he went into the union office and laid his head down on the desk to rest. In a short time, the police caused a fight at one of the gates. The newspapers then gave the story to the public that the strike was out of control.

We gave the second luncheon in honor of Father Maxwell, and many of the priests who had felt that Father Maxwell was a trouble-maker, and had even asked the Bishop to get rid of him, were present. Father Maxwell said: "Some of you have charged this union with being Communist-controlled. It is not true. I know these men, and they are not Communist. However, if seventy-five per cent of them were Communist, I would feel a greater challenge as a man of Christ to be in there fighting and helping to build up the right kind of leadership."

Father Maxwell became an honorary Chaplain of many unions in Buffalo. He died a few years ago, and organized labor lost a great friend.

At this luncheon, action was taken. The priests and the colored ministers who were there signed a resolution urging their people to join this union as being the right kind of union. Many Buffalo unions today have leadership that was inspired at that time. The president of the CIO Council is a Catholic worker, and the vice-president is a Negro.

I stayed on the organizing staff of the union after that experience. We had found how to use new techniques. It troubled some of us a great deal, though, that after our experience, when the organizing staff left, the kind of spiritual fellowship which had started to develop between labor and the churches was often not continued. I am grateful that, several years ago, I was excused from all of my responsibilities of organizing so that I could give all of my time to this matter of the relationship between religion and labor.

I want to tell you a few of the things that we were able to do in the first year's experience with religion and labor fellowship. It started in Columbus, Ohio, where I happened to be living at that time. Hoping to develop a close relationship between labor and religion, we started again with a luncheon. At that time, we asked both religion and labor to be very frank with each other, and, if they had any prejudices, to share them. There was frankness. Labor leaders, who were considered by some of the clergymen to be too radical to be trusted to come into a church, were invited into the churches to speak. Labor leaders who thought that the clergy was a bunch of bosses' stooges found that they were men of vision, and invited the ministers, priests, and rabbis to come to the union halls to speak.

The fellowship continued to have a luncheon meeting once each month. At one meeting, those present had a very frank discussion about the housing situation in Columbus and both the church and labor representatives felt that they could do something about it if they were united. They wanted to form an action group then, but instead they appointed a committee to see just what the need was. They found many groups in the city were interested in housing, and that the need was not for our group to be an organized action group, but to get the various groups together to fight specifically for that one thing. It was found that there had been a rider attached to one of the tax bills in Ohio which made it impossible in the postwar period to have federal housing in the State of Ohio.

A fellowship committee grew into a city and statewide organization. It introduced a bill to make it possible to have federal housing in the state. Religion and labor will feel much more secure as far as private enterprise is concerned if the threat of federal action is there. If private enterprise fails to meet the shelter needs of our people, we will see that we do it through our government.

The Columbus experience has occurred in all sections of the country. Religion and labor in cities and towns throughout the country are getting together once a month, learning to know and to understand each other.

Another field that had not been touched at all was the religious press. Here was a press that we felt should not be biased, should not be controlled. So we became acquainted with the editors of the various religious publications and found a very cooperative reception. Labor articles have appeared in the church press, and they have done much to help church people understand the high aspirations of the labor movement.

For example, a copy of *The Witness,* an Episcopal publication, was recently entitled the "Church and Labor Number." Our brothers in the A. F. of L. were sleeping on the job. They were invited to send articles in, and they did not; all the articles that were sent in by labor were CIO. Some of the reactions to this edition of *The Witness* were interesting. One person wrote, "The last number of *The Witness* delights me. Since I began to go to labor meetings twenty-five years ago as a student of social work, I have known how ignorant the usual middle-class person is of the aims, abilities, and democracy of labor leaders and delegates. I know from my earlier ideas and from the present ideas of my friends—against which I knock my head. Many of the liberal clergy, it seems to me, have also not had the experience really to know what labor leaders are like and are after. I hope the Columbus meetings are going to be duplicated in many other cities."

Here is another one: "If you will refer to *The Witness* of January 25, 90 per cent of it is CIO, and I am not going to 'clear through Sidney.' When I read a church magazine I want to read of the activities of the church and not the activities of a labor union. Therefore, this is your authority to discontinue my subscription."

Another one: "The weekly arrival of *The Witness* always provides one with those moments when I feel exceptionally proud of our church. However, the Church and Labor Number is one of the best ever. Please send me one hundred and eighty copies if they are available for distribution to every family. In the meantime, keep up your sane courage and forthright honesty."

There were very few persons who canceled their subscriptions. I received a letter saying that the board of this publication had asked the editor to set aside one edition a year to carry on this idea.

The Congregational Church, with its *Social Action* magazine for October 15, 1944, also did a very good job in getting the story of religion and labor.

I found that it was very helpful when I could get labor leaders who were in the various churches to write articles to let people know that they were union members as well as church members.

Another thing we found was that people did not know our national leaders. It was hard to get people outside of the unions to know them. I went to Chicago a month in advance to see what opportunities could be opened up to have CIO union leaders speak to religious groups while they were attending the 1944 CIO convention. I sent a questionnaire to the labor leaders, asking them if they would be willing to come a day before the convention assembled to speak to church groups. I had more union men who were willing to speak than I had opportunities. Fourteen of our CIO leaders spoke in fourteen different churches and religious organizations in Chicago before the CIO convention met.

One of the leaders who wrote accepting this invitation indicated that he would prefer to speak to the Society of Friends. I happened to know his story. He had been a Baptist, and when he joined the CIO, he felt for the first time the real challenge of abolishing racial prejudice. He began to teach his Sunday School class accordingly and was ousted as a teacher. He had then left the church. I had an invitation from a Baptist Sunday School to send someone to speak to them, and I sent this man. I did not know that that was the Sunday School which he had left. However, he was accepted; he was glad that he went; they were glad that he came; and the bitterness that he had in his heart was gone.

There are special problems which we are thinking about for the future. I find that many, particularly the workingmen, fear the next few years. They want to know whether there will be jobs enough. It is not that they want the job particularly, for very few people have a job that they like, but they want to have the right to live. The steelworkers' union, in the Little Steel Formula contest with the government, asked for a guaranteed annual wage. That program of ours was handled like a hot potato by management and by government. We have been asking the religious groups what they think about it. We still feel that it has real merit for the economic future of America.

I think that the war proved to us that we have plenty of producers; what we need are consumers. We have solved the problems of production in America, but we have not solved the problems of distribution. In the 1930's, when we talked about a three billion dollar debit to feed the unemployed, people said it would wreck the nation, but now we have spent three hundred billion dollars to feed a war monster. If we had spent one hundred billion dollars in those years to feed our people, I do not believe we would have had a war. I do not believe we are going to continue to have full employment unless we enable our people to be customers. Unemployment insurance, severance pay and a guaranteed minimum annual wage can be used to keep everybody living a wholesome, secure life. Unemployment is something that people fear, but when they are unemployed and do not have fear, they call it leisure. Let us take the fear out of unemployment and turn it into leisure. Furthermore, the guaranteed annual wage given by management will cause management to think in terms of full employment.

The universities grant a sabbatical leave once in a while, I understand. I am advocating a sabbatical leave for everyone. Only, I like to go a little bit farther than the universities. When I take a vacation, it costs me more than to live an ordinary routine life, and so I think we ought to have double pay for that period.

The Negro has been the last one hired and the first one fired; other men who have never had a chance to develop seniority rights to a job and thereby develop the abilities that are within them, have been laid off constantly until finally they became dregs in society. I think that, instead of laying off the underprivileged as we have done in the past, we should keep them working so that they can build seniority and develop the skills that are within them. When there are not enough jobs, let us take the fellows who have been working fifteen or twenty or twenty-five years, and say, "We don't need everybody to work now, so you get a sabbatical leave with double pay." If we had sent ten million of our people on good will tours throughout the world in the 1930's, we would not have had to send ten million of them over there to destroy everything we could produce.

Let us look forward to the future, look upon people and their needs, and uphold their right to live a decent life. It can be done if we give them a decent margin of security. I have enough faith in human nature to feel that if men get a decent break they will do the right thing by it. There may be some who become misfits in society, but, when that happens, a lot of it is our fault. We may have to use some other means to get them to do their share, but, because some people might be slackers, let us not deny society as a whole the right to the good life. The churches have upheld that right.

I am frequently told by members of management, when I talk to them about this, that a man does not live by bread alone. However, Jesus never said that we do not have to have bread in order to live. If we are living the right kind of spiritual life, everyone is going to have enough bread. I do not believe we can separate the spiritual and material life, and have the full life.

From the three great religious faiths, we have these pronouncements upholding this principle: The Rabbinical Assembly of America, in 1934, said: "Wherein Judaism teaches the divine creation of the world, it points explicitly and implicitly to the attitude that God intended the world's resources to be used in the interest of all mankind."

Pope Leo XIII in the encyclical on the condition of labor in 1891 said this: "The blessings of nature and the gifts of grace belong in common to the whole human race."

There are many others I can give, but I want to quote one of the General Assembly of the Presbyterian Church, U.S.A., in 1934: "We recommend that new motives, besides those of money-making and self-interest, be developed in order that we may develop an economic society more consistent with Christian ideals."

Our people do not know that their churches stand for these things, and they have got to know it. These statements came out in a meeting in Columbus where religion spoke to labor. A Jewish rabbi and Catholic priest and Protestant minister gave to labor these social creeds of the churches, and labor said, "That is our program." We forgot that we were of different faiths and that we were representing labor and religion; we were all one. I am sure that when we begin to think together, seeking the social vision, we are going to be one in America and in the world, where all men have the right to live the good life, the abundant life.

III. SPIRITUAL AUTOBIOGRAPHIES OF LABOR LEADERS

XII

THE UNION GIVES JOHN DOE A FACE AND A NAME

BY

MYRNA SIEGENDORF

Chairman of the Community Service Committee, Chicago Industrial Union Council

In telling of why I am in the labor movement, perhaps I ought to say first that motives are a subtle and elusive thing to lay on the table. No matter how rigid we are, our motives today are different from what they were yesterday and will be tomorrow. Today, after some years of direct involvement in the life of the labor movement, my motives for wanting to stay there are somewhat different from what they were seven or eight years ago.

At that time, I was just out of college. Like many other students fresh off the campus, I emerged from an atmosphere tinged in a few spots with shades of liberalism. If I was not sure of myself, you could never have detected it from the tone and volume of voice when I began to defend the justice of organized labor's claims. Of course, my interest there was supercharged with all the emotions of adolescent revolt. My ideas were wet behind the ears, but there was a realistic basis for them in my origins and earlier experiences.

I was born at the end of the First World War in a mill town across the Hudson River from New York City. I do not remember the bitter textile strike of 1926 which the workers lost to the mill owners. Until I left home years later and read a book on labor history, I never heard mention of that strike, nor of what that defeat meant in terms of low wages and sweated conditions of the workers in my open-shop home town. My family lived on a street hemmed in by slums—a merchant's street. I can remember Saturday nights on the street most vividly. On Saturday nights, the store lights went on; families of the working people—Slavs, Poles, and Russians—crowded the street to shop. I remember the faces of the women, made old at thirty with work and the bearing of children. In all those years, especially the years of the Great Depression, poverty, alcohol, and dull despair had settled down upon the people. The merchants ground out their lives pushing pennies across counters. And the slum dwellers eyed them with suspicion and sullen distrust. I could never answer for myself why all of them hung on so tenaciously to lives so empty of hope and laughter and promise. In the street and in the slums you could almost smell the slow decay, the decay of people. And most bitter of all was to see the waste beginning to spread over the faces of the children.

I came from a Jewish family—where Judaism was indifferently accepted. Only my grandmother clung stubbornly to the habits of orthodoxy. Twice a year we were especially reminded of our Jewishness—a day of fasting, and a new dress for the New Year—the unleavened bread of the Passover. The rest of the year, in the epithets and jeers of the Gentile children on the street corners, or coming home from school, you were sometimes reminded that you were different. When death came, the Rabbi swaying over the grave chanted the prayers and your name in Hebrew. But through the days and years, the spiritual satisfactions of this Judaism were meager. This Jewishness did not exclude exploitation of the Negro and contempt for the alien world of the non-Jew.

When I left home the imprint was there. Lacking positive identifications and experiences during those first years away from home, I spent a good deal of emotional energy in the effort to obliterate that imprint. But you cannot repudiate what is part of you. It took time to learn that and to begin the slow process of revaluation and rebuilding.

When I say that motives change, I mean that several years ago I had already acquired certain definite notions about social rights and wrongs. War, poverty, insecurity, human degradation, were wrong. The people's movements mobilized to cut the cancers away were right. I wanted then, as I do now, to be somewhere in the mainstream of the worker's movement. But it is true that the first blush of social conscience had more the color of hostility than understanding, more aggression than insight.

The schools and colleges I attended, the classrooms in which I sat were not decisive in shaping the values I now hold. College living was a thing set apart. I have the impression now of the tidiness of the college campus, its detachment and serenity in the thirties while Europe was being engulfed by fascism and racing toward global war. It seemed as if the curricula had been put together in a vacuum —and then hermetically sealed against the intrusion of those rude realities.

The faculty's talents were energetically applied to teaching the principles of French grammar and how not to speak through the nose. A few professors, sufficiently sensitive to be aware of the world crisis, were themselves frustrated by the intellectual strait-jacketing they received at the hands of the college administrators.

A student had to make a determined effort to break out of the cramped circle of institutional life, and, at the risk of incurring disapproval, to locate the main currents of the world in which he was living. This is by way of explaining that my first encounters with that world were almost wholly extracurricular. I remember one night when Sherwood Eddy was scheduled to speak in a little church in New Brunswick, New Jersey, a group of us obtained permission to go into town to hear him. Sherwood Eddy spoke about the people of America and the way they lived in their dismal cells in the great cities and in the sharecroppers' shacks deep in the South. It was a vivid and moving experience for me.

Several months later, after some of us had organized into a student union, we brought a CIO organizer to the campus to speak. He was an organizer of steelworkers in the days when a steelworkers' union was only a distant but stubborn hope. These were some of the experiences which opened the window for me. And beyond the window lay the broad landscape—broader than the street from which I came, or the college campus to which I had gone, and greener, fresher, holding the bright promise of a better, fuller way of life for all the people.

If formal education, as it was administered, failed to open that window, it also failed to provide the experiences through which the students could achieve what they most sorely required—some degree of emotional maturity. A deep wedge had been driven between scholarship and social action. By default, the college pushed its students into activity. "Doing something" was the way to escape from the ennui of formal education. Students rushed impetuously from one radical enterprise into another. It was a good way to discharge adolescent aggressions, and to do it all in the name of one or another burning cause.

This same type of college product is still emerging annually from our schools and colleges. The educational institution has failed to equip him with a fund of usable information which he can put to work in the laboratory of life. He is not trained to make a contribution along any specific lines. Nor has he been helped to study himself objectively to see how emotional needs and personal frustrations may have conditioned his social outlook. A good many of these people remain armchair generals of the revolution for the rest of their lives. Some go into the labor movement, but are unprepared to cope with what they find there.

There are the martyred intellectuals who feel the need to conceal the obvious fact that their background makes them different from the rank and file of working people. These sometimes go to work in the factories and shops in the attempt to achieve a closer identification with workers. Too many times, they bring along with them a rigid ideological solution to workers' problems—solutions which they hope to fasten upon the unions to which they have attached themselves. Most frequently they fail. And then you have on your hands a cynical fellow—the apostate radical, the tired revolutionary—who has gone sour after a few years in the labor movement, because the workers have not rallied to his battle cry. Though many of them linger on in the unions, they are spiritually isolated and anchorless. And they are embittered.

Perhaps I belabor this point somewhat, because it points up some of the problems and pitfalls which persons like myself meet when we go to work in the labor movement, coming in from the outside, as it were, to find a place and a way in which to function most effectively.

In case what I have said seems to sound like a critique of American institutions of higher learning, let me retrench a bit. I do want to say that I had the good fortune to spend some years doing graduate work in labor economics at the University of Wisconsin before I went to work for the CIO. At the University in Madison, I studied labor history with Selig Perlman, successor to Professor John R. Commons, the first great historian of the American labor movement. Wisconsin helped its students in labor economics to draw closer to political and economic realities. We were taught to dig into the raw materials of economic life, to focus upon the facts, to avoid the dangers and temptations of an arrogant, bone-dry intellectualism.

Perhaps I can best explain this approach to the labor movement by repeating here an excerpt from one of Professor Perlman's articles on the work of John R. Commons:

To Commons, the working men were not abstract building blocks out of which a favored deity called History was to shape the architecture of the new society, but concrete human beings with legitimate ambitions for a higher standard of living, and for more dignity in their lives. As self-determining beings, the workers and their movements were to set their own objectives, their own values, and were entitled to claim from the Intellectuals expert aid in the role they should take to attain the goals set by the leaders risen in their midst. If labor's goals were mutually contradictory, the Intellectual should so inform them. If their objectives were not for the benefit of society and ultimately not for their own, he should tell them that, too.

Commons was a genuine intellectual democrat. These were the principles which guided him throughout his life in his long and various relationships to labor and government. And these were the principles which proved most valuable to me later on.

My first job in the CIO was with Local 20, the Montgomery Ward workers' union in Chicago. I came to Local 20 the year—the first and only year—in which Ward workers enjoyed a union contract with Sewell Avery, ordered by the War Labor Board. In the two years I worked with the Ward workers of Chicago as their education director, I began to understand for the first time the role of the local union in the whole elaborate structure of the labor movement. In its day to day life, in its struggle for survival, I began to appreciate what tremendous energies and voluntary sacrifices go into building a local union. And it was at Local 20 that my values were tested in the crucible of experience.

Working in the labor movement had put me, and those values, on the spot. For the first time, I was in a position of responsibility to people, to large numbers of people whose lives would be directly affected by the wisdom of my judgments and the policies I helped to shape.

The more deeply identified I became with the fight of the Ward workers against the weight of money and power poised against them, the sharper grew my conviction that the labor movement was the most potent weapon the American people have in their struggle for genuine democracy. In their continuous effort to extend economic security to workers and their families, the unions were serving the interests of the entire nation. In the American economy—an economy beset with its deepening crisis, depressions, and mass unemployment—organized labor had come forth with a sound thesis. As a matter of fact, it was the only one that made sense.

It held that we must enlarge the purchasing power of the people so that they may buy back the wealth that they produce. Only through drastic redistribution of income—through higher wages, lower profits, and lower prices—could the economy be saved from stagnation and collapse.

The tragic experience of Europe taught us over and over again the lesson that no society can continue to enjoy the luxury of its political democracy when the masses of people are hungry and without

jobs. Throughout the war and in the postwar years, the labor movement has demonstrated that it is the only people's movement in
America which has given effective expression and leadership to the
democratic aspirations of the people.

When I say that in the labor movement there is the most vigorous
search going on today for the answers to the political and economic
problems of the American people, I do not mean to infer that people
who work for a living are in any way wiser or more virtuous than
any other group in our society. It is just that as workers they have
always been compelled to face the harshest realities. In their struggle
for survival, workers learn that there is no room for wishful thinking. In the fight against their own hunger and insecurity, they are
forced to face concrete facts and to find concrete solutions. This is
one of the healthiest disciplines practiced by the labor movement.

But there are many other processes at work in our unions which
I regard as vital to the survival and extension of our democratic institutions. Out of organized labor's struggle to build a secure movement in a hostile environment has evolved the collective bargaining
process. Out of the most bitter strikes, the violence and the blood-
shed which have characterized American labor history, industrial
governments have emerged through collective bargaining in our
major industries. Around the negotiating tables, a way has been
found to deal with conflicts and wrongs.

Bargaining machinery now extends from the top level where
representatives of management and labor give and take in the process
of defining their mutual rights and responsibilities, down to the bottom where steward and foreman untangle the daily problems arising
in the shop. A more rational exchange has begun to replace grim economic warfare. The labor movement has made a tremendous contribution to the stability and maturation of our democratic institutions by compelling American industry to sit down and bargain. It
has not been easy to secure acquiescence from employers. Most of
the stable collective bargaining relationships which exist today began in turmoil, strikes and lockouts, and were achieved only after
troublesome years of learning how to live together. And it has been
the historic role of the labor movement to seek, demand, and fight

for this more civilized and humane relationship between employer and worker.

An equally significant aspect of the labor movement—and yet one so little understood—is the contribution it makes to the fuller development and creative performance of the individual worker. The vast impersonality of mass production industry has reduced John Doe to anonymity. He is a man with a clock number, operating at the bottom of the pyramid of authority. He takes orders. His value is measured in terms of his productivity. If the management for which he works happens, luckily, to be of the enlightened variety, some consideration may be given to his individual needs and feelings. But this, in our economy, is an aside to the business of profit-making.

The union gives John Doe a face and a name. It gives him a chance to relate himself to people on a cooperative rather than a competitive level. It gives him the opportunity to speak his piece, to take the floor, to turn some of the pressure directed at him back up to the top of the management hierarchy. If he has qualities of natural leadership, he will emerge to take on increasing responsibilities for the welfare of his fellows. He will begin to see his relationship to them, to his community, to the nation and the nations beyond. He is exposed to a process of continuous education and experience which few other institutions in our America of giant industries and giant cities provide.

In the same way, the Johns who make up the following for these natural leaders have a constructive role to play. An almost miraculous transformation often takes place among the workers in a plant after it has been organized. Long stifled fears begin to evaporate. Tensions are reduced. A new healthier adjustment of John to his environment is in the making.

These are some of the values inhering in the labor movement which are most apparent to me as I go about my work within it. I consider it the responsibility of labor leadership to serve as catalysts in stimulating the processes through which these values may be realized. The highest type of leadership is that which not only articulates the needs of the people but also gives guidance in the search for solutions. While giving security to the masses of people, labor leaders must be sufficiently mature and integrated, however, to enjoy working themselves out of the role of domination.

For the unions we build are only as strong as the people who are in them. And no union can long survive as a living instrument of the people if it builds upon their dependency and passivity. The best labor leaders I have seen are invariably those who are most dispensable, for they have been willing to work hard at the difficult and endless job of helping the people to stand on their own feet.

As I think back over some of these developments of insight I am reminded of Arthur Koestler's comment to his readers in his *The Yogi and the Commissar:*

Since my school days I have not ceased to marvel each year at the fool I had been before. Each year brought its own revelations, and each time I could only think with shame and rage of the opinions I had vented before the last initiation. This is still true today, but in a modified form. I am still unable to understand how I was able to bear last year's state of profound ignorance; but lately the new revelations, instead of shattering and destroying all that went before, seem to combine into a pattern sufficiently elastic to absorb the new material and yet with a certain consistency in its basic features.

Similarly, I should be given a chance to change my mind in a few directions, should the labor movement continue to give me new experiences and insights. Nevertheless, I shall hazard a guess that my basic conviction will remain unaltered. And that is the conviction that our American trade unions are the indispensable atoms of our democratic life and that within them lie great reservoirs of energy—the energy of millions of people determined to fight their way out of want and poverty to dignity and security.

XIII

THE BUSINESS OF LIVING IS ALL ONE TRANSACTION

BY

HARRY READ

Executive Assistant to the Secretary-Treasurer, Congress of Industrial Organizations

I am in my present work because I believe in God. That statement may seem startling, coming as it does from a representative of organized labor. You would never decipher that in any of the current newspaper stories; quite the opposite.

I think I can explain by revealing something of my background. I have been a newspaper worker for many years, seventeen of them in the Hearst service, and in the Hearst service I became an executive editor at a very lucrative annual salary. Back in those days, which were the so-called prosperous 1920's when we were all carefully building a depression and starting another war, it was my job to hire and fire reporters. I had a staff of one hundred people working for me on the Chicago *Mirror*.

I had been in exactly the same status as the people who worked for me, having entered the business as a cub reporter and worked for city editors who were unjust, unfair, unreasonable, and overexacting. I think I was a bit fortunate in not having forgotten those times.

About 1928, Mr. Hearst sold to the public a class "A" preferred stock that paid seven per cent. The employees bought certain amounts of this; some a little bit, others quite a lot. After the crash came in 1929, Mr. Hearst was obligated to pay dividends twice a year on that stock.

Along in 1930 there started coming from the publisher's office to me, two or three weeks before each dividend date, a notice that I would have to cut my payroll three or four hundred dollars. That meant I had to call up to that city desk four, five, six, or seven people and say to them, "I am sorry, but I have to lay you off Saturday night."

There was no less work on the paper. These discharges meant that the other members of the staff had to pitch in and do the things that these people had been doing. Seven or eight weeks would elapse, and then I would be permitted to hire back the very people I had laid off. Now, it does not take very much mathematical ability to figure out that the saving of three, four, or five hundred dollars in a week in my single department, and in all of the other departments of the Hearst papers, totals quite a lot. That was a means of piling up a dividend to pay to the owners of the stock. I came to the conclusion, and I have never encountered any evidence to offset it, that Mr. Hearst was paying dividends on his stock by putting his hand into the pockets of the employees and taking out the money. That was the only conclusion I could reach.

Some of the men had been in the employ of that concern for twenty years, had come in young and slowed down, as we all slow down. In the newspaper business, that was cause for dismissal with two weeks' pay in your pocket. The policy of discharging older employees was filling the gutters of this country with broken-down newspapermen who saw nothing to do but drink. Out of that came a great deal of this tradition about drunken newspapermen, though many of them do not drink at all.

In the depression we got a ten per cent cut in pay, and then another ten per cent. That did not concern me particularly because I was making a large salary, but what of the $20 a week copy boy? What of that little fellow who had $2 docked off his pay, reducing it to $18, then another $1.80 taken off three months later, followed by a third cut of ten per cent? It was wholly unilateral on the part of the employer.

In 1936 the Newspaper Guild came to Chicago. At that time I was night city editor of the *Herald Examiner*. People on that staff came to me, for I had the confidence of the people working for me, and they said, "What do you think about this union?" I said, "Join it. By all means, join it."

By 1937 I decided that I was following a rather cowardly course, so in May of that year I joined the union myself. In December, 1938, I led a strike against the Hearst properties in Chicago. It lasted for seventeen months, with much hardship and suffering. There was a tremendous struggle with Mr. Hearst, who was employing gangsters and thugs of all sorts. Shots were fired at our people: little bookkeepers, clerks, copy boys, circulation men, and reporters.

We came out of that, however, with a chain contract with Mr. Hearst. Today that covers all his papers in the country, and the Newspaper Guild now has one of the best contracts in the country with William Randolph Hearst.

Certainly I had more in my mind than merely the injustices that I had seen. What was the principle that actuated me? How do I find myself in the CIO today? What is the thinking of the men with whom I am associated, the various other leaders of the CIO? I will give you the moral background out of which I reason, and the sources from which I derive my thinking, and then I shall assure you most sincerely that the principles which I shall bring to your attention are the basic philosophy of the men in our organization.

Remember that we are dealing with human beings, not with angels. In every Catholic church, every Protestant church, and every synagogue in this land you have a disorderly element of varying size. There is a bad element in every Sunday school, and we also have our bad element. We have men who are unreasonable and unfair, who discriminate against their fellow men, and we have all of the evils that run through society. We have all of them in the labor movement, but we are trying to do something about them, and we try to make our approach as practical as possible.

I am a Catholic. I had been attached to my church. I was the usual run-of-the-mine Catholic, going to church on Sunday, spending about forty minutes there, walking out and considering I had done my job for the week and did not have to worry about it again until the next Sunday. You normally feel kindly disposed toward the fellow next to you. Outside the church, if you step on him and rush away without excusing yourself, or jostle him a bit, or push him around, it is all right. But you do not push him around in church.

So I turned to religion. The thing that struck me was that we have all got into living a life that is compartmentalized. We have split our lives in compartments. In this bin we keep religion; in this bin we keep economics; and in this one our politics. We act as though we could take one set out, exercise it, put it back, and then take out the next set, instead of recognizing that the business of living is all one transaction. So it seemed to me that we should carry into our everyday life our religion, our politics, and our economics all at the same time, and balance them together and base them—on what? Charity? No: first justice, which is an absolutely requisite foundation for charity. There is no such thing as charity without justice. First you do justice, then the door is open for the operation of charity.

Here is a man in clay stained overalls digging in a ditch. A well dressed individual comes by and glances at him and goes on about his business, but then that same man will get up and talk about the dignity of man. He may even go so far as to say that labor is dignified, but if you press him for the explanation, he cannot give it to you.

I think I found the answer to that in the second chapter of Genesis. There I find something that spells out to me why work has dignity. It says, "The Lord God took the man, and put him into the Garden of Eden to dress it and to keep it." That was an injunction laid upon man, "to dress it and to keep it." He was not told specifically how he was to do that. He was given the right of self-determination. We know of the mistake that was made a little later on, and we know the penalty exacted was, "You shall now work and sweat over it." What had been given as a pleasant duty was now made an unpleasant duty, but man was supposed to work prior to the fall of man, as I read Genesis. And of what did the work consist? I believe it consisted of this: that Almighty God made the earth for man, put man on the earth, and then gave him a mission to carry on the work of creation, which is the work of God Himself. Man was to take the earth and improve it; he was to take its products and change their form. It is that element that gives dignity to labor. It does not matter whether a man is digging in the ditch or turning out precious books or painting great pictures, so long as he is improving the work of creation.

I believe that all through the Scriptures we find recognition of this fact that Almighty God Himself wanted men to carry out this mission. You remember the instructions that were given for the building of the Ark and the building of the Temple, how specific they were, and how the best artisans were brought in to do the job. There is constant reference in the Scriptures to the dignity of work and the acclaim that goes to a man who works.

We also find in them the forerunner of all the labor difficulties. I have heard labor say there was a strike in Egypt. It was not a strike. It was a lockout. It was a complaint about unfair labor practices. Pharaoh required the children of Israel to make bricks without straw. We get identically the same thing today on the assembly line: trying to exact work from men that they cannot possibly deliver, that management itself makes it impossible to deliver.

As to violence on the picket line, of course none of us would ever concede that force has any place there. We say that the only time force should be used is to repel force, but let me point out that a man named Moses stepped up on the picket line and killed an Egyptian overseer who was beating one of his colleagues. Moses became a fugitive from justice. He had to flee Pharaoh's wrath in that case, but he killed the Egyptian.

Do you remember how the Jubilee Year was instituted in the Mosaic code? Every fifty years there was a re-distribution. There were rules governing the purchase of a farm, and rules governing the purchase of a house within the city walls. Did you ever ask yourself why those rules were instituted? The only conclusion I can reach is that they were instituted because there were in that community greedy, grasping men, intent on getting all the material possessions in their hands that they possibly could. That was their intention, and so those injunctions were established to restrain the people who proposed to take unto themselves all of the fruits of the earth.

It thrills me to come into a program and find that it is being conducted under the auspices of Jews, Protestants, and Catholics. That is an important thing. It is extremely important to me, because it means that people are working together, and I think Almighty God ordained that we should work together, and meant that we should work together peaceably. That does not mean any invasion of individual prerogative.

A short time ago, I went to one of these intercreedal meetings in Washington. There were present a rabbi, a minister, and a priest, and they got into a round of theological hairsplitting at that meeting, believe it or not. Finally some of the laymen in the audience were called upon to speak, and I got up and said, "Well, it just seems to me that we are off on a tangent here. You know I don't know anything about theology. That isn't my department, and I don't believe any of these lay people out here know anything about it. Now, if you gentlemen have any theological disputes you want to talk about, why don't you talk about them somewhere else. It just seems to me the basis of this meeting should be to avoid areas of disagreement. I happen to belong to the Congress of Industrial Organizations. You see a lot of talk in the newspapers about our disputes with the American Federation of Labor and the Railway Brotherhoods, but all three of our groups have an area of agreement."

When human beings come together, they should determine the things on which they agree, of which there are many more than the things on which they disagree. Having arrived at the area of agreement, they must compromise on the issues that can be compromised, while those on which no compromise is possible must be excluded from the purview of the association. That is the way we organize unions. It is the way we work with the American Federation of Labor.

I have talked to a great many Catholic meetings and am quite active in the field of Catholic associations. Invariably at one of these meetings, somebody stands up and says to me, "Why don't the priests do something about this?" or "Why doesn't the Bishop do something about this?" I have heard Protestants address the same questions to speakers in their groups, and Jews, in their groups. I always answer in this way: "Why don't you do something about it? Why are you sitting around waiting for a clergyman to do your job? It isn't his function to give orders, rush ahead, or push you into this thing. It is up to you to do something about it yourself, and I think I am safe in saying that if you will do that you will find the clergyman right beside you." I have seen bishops, rabbis, ministers, and priests take a stand on these social problems to the point where the rocks started to fly, and when they looked around, they did not have any troops with them. They were left alone with nobody giving them any support.

That is not the way the job is to be done. I think it is extremely necessary for everybody to promulgate the doctrines on the dignity of work and the moral reason that underlies them. I believe we have got to abandon the old concept that force alone decides issues. The trouble with force is that if you do not keep applying it, the other fellow gets strong enough to come back and use a little of his own.

That is what has been going on in the world. We have tried to solve our problems by main strength instead of by moral principles. We have to change our ways. We shall not do it by groups. We have got to do it individually. The only way I can insist that my government live up to its obligations in the world is by living up to my own obligations. Then I am in a position to apply pressure. I cannot go out and do as I please among my fellow men, and then insist that my government do the right thing. We have all got to get back to the individual basis. We have to recognize in one another the fact that we are all children of the same God. I think if we can recognize the fatherhood of God, we will not have so much trouble recognizing the brotherhood of man.

XIV

LABOR RELATIONS ARE HUMAN RELATIONS

BY

ALFRED HOFFMANN

First Vice-President, American Federation of Hosiery Workers

I happen to be one of those individuals who were born into the labor movement. I was "brung up" in it. I was raised on the wrong side of the railroad tracks in the city of Milwaukee, where I associated almost daily with railroad men coming and going from work. Then, as my parents moved up the social scale, we moved out of the railroad district into the brewery town in Milwaukee, and I spent most of my youth playing cops and robbers, cowboys and Indians, on Pabst Brewing Company property where we were allowed to run loose as long as we did not get too noisy and disturb the brewmaster.

From early childhood, unions were normal to me, like getting up in the morning and going to school. There was a skilled craftsman or brewery worker of one type or another in every family in the neighborhood and they all belonged to the union, and they all wore their union buttons on their caps. In the particular section of town where I lived, union dues were collected in some of the taprooms, so that people in the neighborhood did not have to go downtown to pay their union dues. I just soaked up the spirit of unionism along with soot and cobblestones.

My mother was forced to go to work in a nonunion sweater plant about the time I was eight years old, and from then on I was put on my own in respect to shouldering responsibility. I became a first-class housemaid, got to be a second-class cook by getting suppers ready, while my lunch hour at school was taken up with ten minutes of eating and fifty minutes of drying dishes in a restaurant.

I have always worked. I do not remember any time when I have not worked. In running errands, walking dogs, peddling papers, going to fruit camps in northern Michigan and working on farms, I found that, if I needed any pocket money, I had to earn it, and it was a good thing for me. The environment I came out of forced me to work and forced me to develop opinions regarding trade unions and social organization.

As I look back now on the public school I attended, I marvel at the job that was done. We had a large Negro group; we had the largest Chinese group in Milwaukee; we had people representing every race and nationality—and we got along fine. In the high school through which I worked my way, we had the same sort of mixture.

One thing I look back on very fondly today is our attitude toward religion. When Freddie's sister was trying to win a prize in the Baptist Sunday school, the whole neighborhood turned out to help her. We all joined the Baptist Sunday School: Catholic, Jew, Protestant, and unchurched. Then out of respect to those who were members of the Catholic Church, we all made eleven o'clock Mass, so that our attention to religion was universal in aspect.

As far as religious influence in my own home was concerned, I recall violent arguments my father had with his neighbors, although he died while I was still very young. He was antichurch. My mother was personally a deeply religious woman, though against the church as an institution. I was told, at about the time I was ready to walk, that I was free to look for my own preference.

When I finished high school, I had the first big battle with my mother. With her German background, she insisted that, "You are the right age now to learn a skilled trade." I said, "No, I want to go to the University of Wisconsin and become an economist." She said, "You have got plenty of time to become an economist after you have served your apprenticeship." That was one of the first major battles where I took a lacing. I went into a factory and learned full-fashioned knitting, and qualified myself as a journeyman.

Having soaked up unionism before I ever went to work, the first day on the job as an apprentice I looked up the shop steward and wanted to know when I could join the union. He almost fell from his knitting machine. He had never had that experience before. Immediately upon joining the union, I became active in its work. I was exactly eighteen years old when first elected a delegate to the Hosiery Workers' convention.

At the time I joined the hosiery workers, the entire national organization had about nine thousand people in it. It was a craft union, taking into membership journeymen and apprentices. It was a small union, a young union, and a thoroughly democratic union. We were so democratic that we did not even believe in a paid president. We believed in a paid secretary, as in the old German trade union system, but the president's position was strictly honorary.

As I said, I had always wanted to become an economist. Thank goodness, I became a knitter first. I decided, after I had worked as a journeyman for about a year and a half, that I needed more education, so I turned toward Brookwood Labor College, which was then a labor school at Katonah, New York. I corresponded with the college and made arrangements to attend. Our national union discovered that I had made these arrangements, and at their annual convention decided to give me a scholarship to the school. I took advantage of the offer.

After a year at Brookwood Labor College, I came back to Milwaukee to go to work. I had gained an awful lot of weight at Brookwood. All the students had to do physical labor, and I had worked on the road-rolling crew and as a cook. When I got to Milwaukee to go to work on a knitting machine, I discovered that the alleyways were uncomfortably narrow, so the foreman told me that I ought to wait until they got a machine with a nice, wide aisle. Until this machine was ready, I went out into the harvest fields and worked as a farm hand with a threshing crew.

Shortly thereafter, I was elected to the field staff of the union. Our union was so democratic that it did not even appoint organizers. We elected them at conventions. The organizers were responsible only to the convention. If the secretary or treasurer told you to do something, you did not have to do it. You could take your case to the convention if anything were said about it.

Having been elected, I was shipped into one place where you can get a second good education. I was shipped south in 1927. In that period there was no National Labor Relations Board, and there was no Wagner Act. Unions had no status, and it was a matter of getting along through self-preservation. If you will recall, that was the era of gangsterism, of aggressiveness, and I started out organizing with one thought and ideal in mind.

It was that of class-consciousness. That was the thing that had driven me from the time I went to work in the factory. I did not want to associate with any but working people. None but working people were worth associating with. I could appraise the status and the function of the middle class in our society. I had absolutely no use for anybody with money; whether he had inherited it or stolen it made no difference to me. He was a parasite.

I started out with a good Socialist philosophy. I studied Communism very carefully. I studied the IWW and its philosophy. I had studied anarchism and Nihilism, and rejected them and the other philosophies. But I had to mix up just a little bit of gangsterism with my pure Socialism in order to survive in the South.

It was in that period that I think I stepped out of the freshman class. During four years, I was embroiled in possibly three hundred strike situations, and had as many as forty-five thousand people on the strike front in the cotton textile industry. It was during that period of hammering that I moved into the sophomore class. I matriculated in some very fine penal institutions during these years, and conducted labor business as usual while I was locked up.

After having spent four years in the South, I was brought into an area of Pennsylvania, at that time just as tough, in counties like Bucks, Monroe, Montgomery. There the nature of the work I was doing was changed; and with the change in the nature of the work, my concept of the whole problem of labor relations began to change. Up until that time, all I had to do was get up on a soap box, just drip vitriol, call the boss anything in the world, keep the people steamed up, run a good strike, and somebody else would come along and settle it. I could not have settled a strike in those days for love or money.

Mr. Ed McGrady, who is now with RCA Victor as vice-president, used to come into these situations to settle them, along with myself and A. N. Weinstock of the United States Conciliation Service. In this second phase of my development, I had to sit down with employers and settle grievances. Then it dawned on me that employers were human beings. The same things that made my hackles rise made their hackles rise, so that, for me at least, for the first time human relations became a part of labor relations. Up until that time human relations had no part; I had thought I was entirely objective.

Now I know better. In our particular industry we are cursed and blessed with a large number of small producing units. We have over nine hundred and seventy-five plants and our total employment at the moment is about one hundred twenty-five thousand people. We have a large amount of owner management, and even where we do not have owner management, I think there is a good sized segment of management men who are fully aware of human relations. Among the employers that I do business with, I have taken the time to study their idiosyncrasies. They are used to my tone of voice on the telephone. I am allergic to a telephone, and so am very disagreeable on it, but they are used to that. So also, when I am sitting down with an employer who has stomach ulcers and has to lie down after he gets a hot meal, I do not try to run a conference through the noon hour. If I am doing business with an employer who happens to have a death in the family and has to leave at four o'clock, I respect his departure time. That type of mutual respect is widespread in our industry.

In the city of Philadelphia we have been very fortunate because of the influence of the Friends. The Friends for years have been arranging small group meetings between Quaker employers and labor people. I remember one of these conferences where Mr. Horace Potts, of Potts Iron and Steel, got in the corner with the chief shop steward, a girl who was one of our hosiery workers, and they got to talking. He had a bitter complaint about a shop steward in her plant, and this girl had a bitter complaint to make about a wild eyed partner in the business. When they left, they were the closest buddies. They had talked in the corner that whole evening.

In the industries in which there has been collective bargaining for any length of time, there is a good healthy mutual respect between labor and employers, which expresses itself in the attitude of the representatives who do the talking. It is a healthy respect, and that is why I am not at all pessimistic about the future of labor relations in this country.

While working in the furnace of the South, something else happened. I ran into two types of situations: one in which organized religion was actively fighting labor and labor organizers; and the second, in which organized religion was siding with labor openly and frankly. In several situations I ran up against very learned orators, with theological seminary diplomas, whom I had to combat by preaching sermons. I could not make labor speeches. I just simply had to take the Bible, interpret it, and quote from it. At that time, I became a very close student of the Bible. My old annotated copy is full of notes. There are sections of it almost worn out, particularly the Book of James.

About 1935, the union decided that I had talent for research, so I was taken off the road entirely and put into the office, handling research and administering one entire section of the industry.

In the meantime, something else very serious happened to me. I got married in 1934, and the most wild eyed organizer and the most wild agitator starts to tame down after he is married. I met my wife in an organizing campaign. She was a hosiery mill worker, and I started a very ardent campaign of seven months. I did not think I was ever going to make the grade. I finally broke down her resistance: she said, "Yes."

In 1937, I became very much aware of the bankruptcy of trying to live by bread and meat alone. Of my own volition, I began to look for something to satisfy the spiritual hunger, and out of all the institutions to pick, I picked the Presbyterian Church.

After about three and one half years of working in the South, I had become very conscious of the bankruptcy and the starved condition of my manner of living. I lived in a hotel. Practically all of my waking time was devoted to the job. To be sure, my social life was part of the job, and I was not ostracized by the community, even in the southern towns. I found all through the South, particularly in cities of over twenty-five thousand population, transplanted persons, businessmen, professional men, people of a middle-class group, who were broadminded and liberal and welcomed me into their homes, so that I could not say that I was starved from the point of view of social contacts. But I became conscious of the fact that my manner of living was not normal. There were a lot of things that the ordinary fellow on the street was enjoying—for instance, fishing and vacations—that I was losing out on; and without doing anything about it consciously, there were moments when I would sit in my hotel room and think those things over. That particular state of affairs corrected itself to a large extent when I came north.

I have come to a number of personal conclusions, as a result of almost twenty years in the labor movement, with respect to people who are doing the kind of work I have been doing. I have come to the conclusion that the man or woman in organized labor who does not maintain a real sense of humor can end in only one of two ways: either he will end as a dyed-in-the-wool extreme leftist, or he will end in an insane asylum—one or the other, there is no middle course. I have run into a number of people in organized labor who have no interest except the labor movement, and who do, nevertheless, maintain a sense of humor. But, somewhere along the road, they have forgotten how to relax, how to play, and have absolutely no interest except eating their job, living their job, and doing their job. I would say that those people are geniuses. They are doing the best job in organized labor, but what they are doing to their personal lives is abominable. In no instance where that has taken place have I seen any home life, nor can I say that the people involved are entirely well balanced. It is awfully hard to keep that sense of humor under certain circumstances, but it is an essential.

Secondly, I have come to the conclusion that this whole strange field of labor relations, whether it is at the shop level or at the national level, is a matter of human relations and only human relations. Most of us in the labor movement have concluded that the type of fanaticism which maintains that organized labor can be the beginning and end of all things for those who work, is just a lot of nonsense.

The labor movements can cater to the material welfare of people. They can give back to people who work in mass production industry some sense of dignity, some sense of personality; but they cannot replace or substitute for other things in the worker's spiritual life. During the past five years, certain interests have tried to enlist me in promulgating class religion; but I objected, because I cannot picture class in religion. I see it, but I cannot picture it from the point of view of pure theology. If the concept of labor relations is also that of human relations, I think that we, in our union, are on the right track, because one of the fundamentals that we drum home to members of the field staff is this: the same thing that gets your hackles up gets the other fellow's hackles up: the same treatment that you cannot stand, he cannot stand; and if you will just remember that when you are doing business with the other fellow, you will do most of your business across the table and little on the picket line. I will be frank and say that I had to learn that lesson the hard way. I had to learn it on hundreds of picket lines. Now I am trying to shortcut the job for the other fellows working with us.

One other thing I would like to point out is that we Americans have a very unfortunate habit of wanting all of our news hot, fresh, and fast. We have to have it in capsules just as fast as it happens, and once the radio announcer has given us the headlines of world-shattering news compressed into three minutes, plus two minutes of commercials, we never take the time to review it. So we are becoming instant-minded.

I want to impart to you a little of my callousness in respect to short-term trends, whether those short-term trends affect the labor movement or world history. The rash of strikes we have had since V-J Day is a very natural thing. People are mentally muddled, morally muddled, and financially muddled from the impact of what happened during five years of war. These strikes, as far as I can see, were the escaping steam coming out of the safety valve. We had the same type of thing after World War I. We had practically the same thing on a very small scale after the Civil War. All we have to do is view these things in terms of long trends.

The fact of one individual union basing the request for wage increases on ability to pay does not make the labor movement socialistic or communistic. I get a very expensive service in my office. In it appears a weekly analysis of new labor contracts negotiated with industry. It revealed that while we were upset by the General Motors dispute, the oil strike, the steel strike, and the meat packers' walkout, thousands and thousands of labor agreements were negotiated and executed without any work stoppages. Contracts for the entire ladies' and men's garment industry were negotiated without work stoppage. The whole hosiery industry negotiated a two year contract with one work stoppage, and that was at a small plant in Georgia. Organized labor as such had not changed its philosophy.

Another thing of which I find it very difficult to convince people is that Joe Doakes who belongs to the union is: number one, a citizen; number two, a resident of a normal community like mine, Willow Grove, outside of Philadelphia; number three, a taxpayer and home owner, who belongs, as I do, to the Third Ward Civic Improvement Association, and who might, if he is an officer, get an invitation to belong to the Chamber of Commerce to represent labor, as I have. He is a member, in seven cases out of ten, of some religious denomination, his kids go to school, and his wife belongs to the Parent-Teacher Association. He is just like anybody else: that is, if he is working in a plant in which management is trying to fight labor, he is radical, he wants to fight back; if he is working in a plant where labor relations have settled down, he wants wise, stable leadership, and that is the kind of leadership he elects. During depressions, he wants the very wisest kind of leadership he can find, the kind that is going to save industry and work out programs to provide jobs.

I am grateful for one thing in my experience, and that is that I had the opportunity of learning my economics on a practical basis instead of on a theoretical basis. After I had seen some of the practical problems, I studied theory and could be very sympathetic with it because I knew the fundamentals from experience. In the same manner, I am grateful that I came out of a family in which religion was not administered to me with castor oil, and that I was able to seek my own level rather than be dragged to it. I was moved by my own experience in that respect.

XV

I TURNED TO SOCIAL ACTION
RIGHT AT HOME

BY

LUCY RANDOLPH MASON

Southern Public Relations Representative, Congress of Industrial Organizations

My earliest recollection of considering an immortal destiny and the relationship of life thereto takes me back to about the age of five. I was sitting on the stone step of my father's study in Shepherdstown, West Virginia, enjoying the spring sun when a chill of fear smote me. Where would I go when I died? Assuredly father and mother would "go to heaven," and unless I went there, too, I would be a lonely waif in eternity. I had no fear of "hell" in itself, but was mortally afraid of being separated from my parents.

Pondering this problem, I decided we go where we want to go. If one wanted "to be good and go to heaven," one would live that way. Then and there I decided once for all where I wanted to go.

The second religious problem I can recall presented itself as I was walking down the lane behind our house when I was about seven. It arose from the often repeated words in the Episcopal service, "forever and ever." How could even God be forever and ever? Then it flashed through my mind that, if there were not "forever and ever," what was there before the beginning, and what would be after the end? That question being just as difficult as the one about eternity, another problem was settled.

There must have been an early budding of some sort of social conscience, for my great-aunt told me in later life that, when I was a very small child, I insisted on praying for the devil. When asked why, I said, "He is so bad he must be very unhappy, and I want to ask God to make him good."

Father was an Episcopal minister; mother, the daughter of one. They were deeply good, sincerely spiritual, and most humanely kind. Their theology included social ethics. At times, mother carried her religion into crusades to right wrongs. She exposed horrors in the Virginia penitentiary long before that institution was finally made modern and humane. After spending a night in the Richmond city jail to help a distraught girl who had tried to commit suicide, mother gave the newspapers her impression of that ill-kept and filthy place. Her great heart went out to everyone in distress, from a repentant thief just out of the penitentiary, to an outcast leper in India. Many a newly liberated convict came to stay in our home, and mother founded the Richmond branch of the Mission to Lepers. So it was natural that I drew inspiration from the social thunderings of the Hebrew prophets in the Old Testament, and from Jesus' insistence that love of man was inseparable from love of God.

In my early twenties, Walter Rauschenbusch and other modern prophets of a better social order had a profound effect on me. More and more, religion became related to social action. Florence Simms, industrial secretary of the national Young Women's Christian Association, speaking of her experience, said something that was applicable to mine: "I realized that personal goodness is not enough. There must be a passion for social justice." It gradually dawned on me through the years that one could not have a real conception of God unless one aspired to "love one's neighbor as oneself," and desired the good life for all people. Dr. William Ernest Hocking, in *The Meaning of God in Human Experience,* expresses this in a sentence I have loved since first coming across it. Essentially it was this: "Some men find their way to God through man, and some men find their way to man through God; but no man is complete until he has found his way to both God and man."

These things have been very real to me. Religion has drawn me to my fellow man and linked me to eternity. It is difficult to say what I want to express, but it is so intimately a part of my spiritual autobiography that I must essay it. I cannot separate the ideal of loving God with all my being from loving my brother as myself. In every great emotional experience, whether of joy or sorrow, the barriers separating me from God and man have seemed to dissolve and I have known what the words *identity* and *unity* can mean in the soul's experience. Conjoined with this experience, there is a perception of eternity, and even in the here and now I sense immortality.

In my teens I dreamed of being a foreign missionary, and in my twenties I turned to social action right at home. I saw how boys and girls, going into industry at pittance wages and working ten or more hours a day, grew old and worn while still young in years. Naturally, I became a believer in labor unions. One winter during a streetcar operators' strike, I would not board a car, and walked many miles, sometimes in snow and rain, to and from the law office where I worked as a stenographer and to other destinations. Social leanings made me active in the cause of woman suffrage and, later, in the League of Women Voters. For a time I was president of the Richmond units of these two organizations. I felt women had a special responsibility to humanize politics and legislation. Groups of us frequently went to the state legislature to lobby for child welfare bills and for social and labor legislation.

Only one organized group of men in Virginia supported us in these things, the State Federation of Labor. Individual ministers and other men sometimes went with us, but they were the exceptions. So I learned to look to labor unions for support of social measures.

First as industrial secretary, and later as general secretary, of the Richmond YWCA, and as a volunteer in many other civic and social organizations, my life became very full of social action. A concern for fair play and justice to Negroes and for more understanding and good will between the races led me into many activities in this field. As a member of the executive committee of the Virginia Commission for Interracial Cooperation, I took part in some exciting battles on state laws discriminating against Negroes. Richard Carrington, then president of the Virginia Commission, and I bore the brunt of hot fights in the City Council over a segregation ordinance and for Negro parks and playgrounds. Never have more bitter invectives been hurled at me than during those Council hearings.

The National Consumers' League gave me an opportunity to work on a national scale for the things about which I had been concerned in my native state. I went to New York as the League's general secretary in 1932, a very exciting period for an organization which expressed a concern for good working conditions through state and federal legislation. Founded by religious and civic leaders and led through most of its history by that great crusader, Florence Kelley, the League had been the originator of minimum wage laws in the United States. In 1932, under the leadership of Mary W. Dewson, the League renewed with great success the fight for state minimum wage laws. The present Federal Fair Labor Practices Act was drafted by Benjamin V. Cohen, the League's unpaid counsel, who also drafted the state bills passed in 1933 and thereafter.

Five years with the Consumers' League brought close contact with many labor union leaders, some of whom were among the founders of the Committee for Industrial Organization. Also, I had the opportunity to meet many socially minded people in my travels through the eastern, southern, and central states.

From its inception, I saw in the Committee for Industrial Organization economic salvation for the unorganized masses of American workers. Here was social action founded on principles of brotherhood. Here was a movement which opened doors of opportunity to depressed and exploited wage earners. To women and minority groups, it said, there shall be no discriminations. It was committed to a policy of equal pay for equal work.

When given the opportunity in 1937 to join the CIO staff as southern public relations representative, I eagerly accepted. The spiritual and social, as well as the economic, significance of this organization was manifest to me from the beginning. Nine years with the CIO have brought me that deep satisfaction which comes from being a part of a great movement for human welfare.

It would be impossible to write my spiritual autobiography without trying to interpret what the CIO means to me. Here is that great movement as I believed it to be nine years ago, and as I know it to be now.

There was nothing more obvious on the American scene in 1932 than the need for industrial unions in mass production industries. Indeed, as pointed out by many observers of the times, industrial unionism was long overdue. Even the impetus given by the first federal efforts to aid workers in organizing could not be used successfully by craft unions trying to organize the steel, automobile, and other basic industries.

The times called for industrial unions which would bring the combined strength of all workers in a plant or industry into one powerful union. The Committee for Industrial Organization, first organized in November, 1935, set out to do just that. By 1937, it had gone far along this road, and in 1938 it held a constitutional convention from which emerged the Congress of Industrial Organizations.

The basic concept of mutual dependence in industrial unions is akin to the religious demand for practicing brotherhood. A common bond is created between the most skilled craftsman in a plant and the common laborer. An interdependence of interest grows up between the best paid and the poorest paid workers. The special bargaining power of the skilled is linked with the mass power of the greater number of semiskilled and unskilled. All workers in the industry must be organized and protected without discrimination because of race, religion, or sex. There must be a fair distribution of wages to each group according to its skills, but the least skilled workers must be adequately paid for the essential labor they perform. On these principles the CIO was organized.

When church people express regret that the CIO split from the American Federation of Labor, I ask if they think it unfortunate that the Methodists left the Church of England. As the Methodists brought fresh air and new life to organized religion, so the CIO brought new vitality and vigor to the labor movement. The birth of the CIO was as inevitable and as desirable in the economic field as was that of the Methodists in the religious field. There is a kind of kinship, too, in that both these movements reached out to the common people.

The CIO has succeeded because it is founded on sound principles. It has built a membership of six million and become the dominant organization in mass production industries. It has raised living standards for millions of hitherto economically submerged people. It has improved the economic situation of women workers and of minority groups and races. It has had a wholesome effect on the entire labor movement, stimulating other unions to more activity, and in some instances to more fair and inclusive membership practices.

In 1937 I heard a distinguished Baptist professor of theology say to a YMCA and YWCA student conference, "Fifteen years from now people will probably look back to the beginning of the CIO and realize that the churches should have helped this movement to lift the submerged masses of America." Many people now think that prophecy was a true one.

From its earliest days, organized labor has shown concern for matters beyond the immediate union objectives of better wages, shorter hours, and improved working conditions. This was natural, because "labor" represents workingmen and women and their children: it is a large section of the people. There are now more than fourteen million members of all branches of organized labor, who, with their families, constitute about one third of the population.

The Congress of Industrial Organizations has surpassed all other bodies of organized workers in promoting a socially desirable program for the common good. Mr. John Paul Jones, an Atlanta businessman and member of the Episcopal Church, whom I first met at a church forum, has expressed this so well that I quote from a letter he wrote me recently. He said:

The CIO is the only intelligently organized, large, militant force in America today actively campaigning for the good of the common people. That they serve their own ends does not detract from their already great and growing contribution to human welfare.

It is one of the most encouraging signs of the times that this vast body of American working people should have so broad and sound a conception of labor's part in American and world affairs.

Some of the measures supported by the CIO show a deep concern on the part of industrial workers for farmers and the rest of society. These measures show, too, a concern for preservation of the nation's resources so that future generations may inherit a good earth and live in peace and security. Briefly condensed, here are some of the things the CIO supports: the Farm Security Administration; soil and forest conservation; long-term, low-interest loans to farmers; farm cooperatives; parity prices for farm products; extension of social security benefits to farm people; a Missouri Valley Authority along TVA lines, and other similar river valley authorities; a national housing program to meet the needs of city, town, and rural people, and especially for ex-service men; a more inclusive social security program, with higher benefits; provision for medical and hospital care; maternal and child care; federal aid to education, and for school lunches; a permanent Fair Employment Practice Commission; greater opportunity for education and economic security.

The CIO is deeply concerned with international cooperation and world security. It has supported all measures looking to the creation of the United Nations, and for helping people everywhere to gain a higher standard of living. It has supported all appropriations for UNRRA. In an official statement on atomic energy the CIO advocated:

Suitable international machinery . . . to bring the use of atomic energy under world-wide social direction. . . . United Nations control of atomic energy for military purposes, and all production of atomic bombs. United Nations control of atomic energy raw materials and production everywhere in the world, with full authority to inspect, investigate and police. . . . Complete public control of all atomic energy patent rights and licenses in the United States.

In its entire program the CIO seems to recognize a brotherhood of man that is worldwide in scope. Here, too, there is kinship to the religious concept of universal brotherhood.

As a Southerner with a long concern for seeing the South converted from "The Nation's Economic Problem No. 1" to a rich producing and consuming region, I have rejoiced in the spread of industrial unions there. Materially, the CIO has improved the economic status of countless thousands of people, and has enriched communities by the increased purchasing power of wage earners. At the same time a new dignity and self-respect have come to these organized workers, both white and Negro, through their collective strength. At work, they cannot be unjustly shoved around by autocratic foremen. In the community, they count as citizens and participate in community life as never before. The unions have something in common with the fundamental demand of religion that human personality be respected.

During the nine years since the CIO came South, it has been intensely interesting to watch the development of political activity on the part of Southern workers, who previously had been largely ignored by politicians because so few of them voted. In many towns, the first deliberate organized effort to use ballots has been for self-defense. Union members combined their votes to oust brutal sheriffs who denied people their civil rights and helped employers fight unions. This experience of gaining civil rights through voting naturally led to wider use of the ballot to promote workers' interests on a larger scale. There are encouraging signs throughout the region that workers' votes will increasingly help elect more intelligent and progressive men to state legislatures and to Congress. The instances in which this has already happened are indicative of what can be expected in the future. This is a development in accord with religious ideals, as democracy is founded on the worth and dignity of the individual, a concept that grew out of religious teachings.

The CIO has done more to raise the economic and civil status of the Negro in the South and to improve race relations than any other organization. In states where the white primary has kept Negroes from voting in what were the real elections, industrial unions advocate primaries open to both races and encourage their Negro members to register and vote. Many church people wish that organized religion would be as aggressive and realistic as the CIO in promoting justice, citizenship, and economic opportunity for Negroes.

The South is a region of churches, big and little, and of many small sects. Religion has an appeal to a large part of the population. Unions are chiefly made up of church members, and nearly all union meetings are opened with prayer. It is customary for local unions to have their own chaplains, usually lay preachers who work in the plants. Some of the most genuine and appropriate prayers I have heard have come from union men at these meetings. Surely here is a common interest between churches and unions which should be developed to the mutual interest of both. Yet most church people outside the labor movement have not the slightest conception of the spiritual motivation to be found in union members and leaders.

"Because I wanted to do the greatest good for the greatest number of people in the shortest time," was the answer given by Steve Nance, of Georgia, when a friend asked why he had left the presidency of the State Federation of Labor to direct the southern organizing campaign of CIO textile and garment unions. When he died of overwork just a year after the drive began, his funeral service was shared by his own Baptist pastor and a Methodist minister long close to him.

The Baptist minister said:

I never knew Steve called on to do something to aid humanity that he was not there to do his part. He felt he had a mission and what God had given him to do was to help as many workingmen and women as he could. His whole life was wrapped up in a desire to help men.

The Methodist minister said:

I am as sure that Steve Nance was a called man as I am that Moses was a called man, and I am as sure that in his own mind and heart, every step was taken and measured for the good of those whom he was called to serve. . . . This quiet, rugged man's greatest service was rendered in the cause of organized labor, and to that he was true, even unto the end.

I have quoted these tributes because they are applicable to many other leaders of labor, and many a man and woman in the union rank and file.

With its broad program, it is natural that the CIO has attracted many people with strong social and religious motivation. Ministers, rabbis, college professors, social workers, and young men and women fresh from college, have come into the CIO as organizers, executives, researchers, publicists, and office workers. The ideals which bring these professional people into the labor movement are beautifully expressed by Bernard Borah in letters written to me while he was in the Army. Bernard was a graduate of the University of Tennessee who chose the CIO as his field of service and was outstanding among young southern union leaders. In one letter written at a time when the war was not going well, he said:

The war and the labor movement are alike in teaching patience: you must keep fighting, paying little attention to successes or failures along the road; keeping your equilibrium and your good sense and your passion for justice, and your diligence, because after all the last battle and the whole war are the important things.

In a letter written a week before his death in an Army hospital where he was awaiting the operation under which he died, Bernard wrote:

The man who feels God in the universe and cannot explain Him or describe Him, but accepts Him without worrying about it . . . the man who realizes that if there is a heaven one can be sure of it only if we build with our own sweat and blood and brains on earth—the man who admires and loves goodness for itself alone, and who sees within man an ageless spirit, warm and good, seeking a good life—a man who loves man, and loves life, and loves justice—then to this man life becomes more important than death, and he must strive to do good and build goodness on earth.

This educated and articulate young labor leader and soldier has expressed what I am convinced lies deep in the heart and soul of many a union man and woman. I can personally testify that, if all my life had been spent for the sole purpose of preparing for these nine years with the CIO, it would have been richly worth living.

Life was full of zest and interest before 1937, but this period has been the most spiritually rewarding of all.

It is now well established that there is possible an economy of abundance. The world has enough natural resources, scientific knowledge, and workers' skills to provide decent living for all people everywhere. A Florida school superintendent well expressed this when he said to a conference:

Jesus would pray today: "We thank Thee for our daily bread; give us the sense to distribute it."

That is the problem for modern men to solve: how to distribute what we can so richly have. The unions of the Congress of Industrial Organizations, and most of organized labor, struggle to bring about the answer to such a prayer by securing a more equitable distribution of America's potential abundance.

It would be well if the Church and Synagogue, in addition to teaching the spiritual verities in which we live and move and have our being, would draw closer to the labor movement and share more of its concern for the welfare of the men, women, and children who make up its ranks. Religion can enrich and bless union members, giving them new spiritual insights, provided the Church and Synagogue capture more of the prophetic vision.

XVI

I HAVE FOUND IN CONFLICTS A PEACE

BY

NELSON H. CRUIKSHANK

Director, Social Insurance Activities, American Federation of Labor

I was born in the small town of Fostoria in northern Ohio. My father and mother were both native-born Americans. My mother's ancestral line goes back, no one knows how far, into Virginia history, while my father was of the third generation of Scotch and English immigrants. My father was a businessman engaged at the time of my birth in operating a grain elevator.

Both parents were deeply religious. The atmosphere of our home was genuinely religious in the very best and highest sense of the word. To this religious atmosphere and heritage I shall always owe a great deal. It was not only a religious piety, but an intellectually liberal religion. My father, I always felt, was miscast in the role of businessman. He was by nature a scholar, much more one than any of his children ever proved to be. Even in the midst of an active business life he enjoyed reading his Greek New Testament prior to teaching the young men's Sunday school class of which he had charge all his life. He engaged in active work in the YMCA.

Also he had an unusually liberal attitude toward labor. Just one instance I shall give illustrates that. In central Ohio there were then, and still are to some extent, what were known as revival meetings in the church. At the time of one of these interdenominational meetings, there were handbills printed for advertising purposes. When the committee brought the handbills to my father, he said, "We can't use these." Someone said, "What is the matter?" My father said, "We don't use any printing in my church that does not have the union label on it." Where he got the idea that organized labor was something that had a legitimate place in the economy, back as early as 1912 and 1914, I do not know, except that his mind was one that was always reaching out into the social and ethical implications of his religious teaching and his own religious studies.

My uncle told me, years after the event, that at one time he heard on the floor of the Produce Exchange in Toledo, of which body he and several of his brothers were members, that there was a move under way to combine in order to fix grain prices throughout northern Ohio. My uncle told me that my father stood on the floor of the Produce Exchange and said, "Gentlemen, you can force me out of business. You can force me out of your association, but you cannot force me into an unfair combination. Our business runs on the principle of free competition, and if this thing goes through, my last dollar will go to exposing what happened in the secret and executive meetings of this exchange."

That kind of spirit, that kind of philosophy, and that kind of willingness to carry high ideals into business relationships created the atmosphere in which I grew up. All my life, I shall be trying to live up to the standards that were set for me at home, for these attitudes my mother also fully shared.

With this, my father also had a kind of stern Puritanism that made him feel it was highly essential that his son should learn what it meant to work. During the time I grew up, there was no necessity to contribute to the family budget; but I remember how often he told me and others that he thought one of the finest things that he got out of study of the Old Testament was the Jewish tradition that every boy should learn a trade and know how to take care of himself. Even if he went into business or professional life, the work experience would be valuable background.

Consequently, I was encouraged to spend vacations, after-school hours, and other free time in learning what a day's work was. At the age of fourteen I was working in factories. My high school was an industrial high school. There I learned to operate machines, so I was able to go into the automobile factories in Fostoria and

Toledo. Later I worked as a truck driver and had three seasons as a seaman on the Great Lakes. By dint of hard labor and devotion to the task, I was enabled to get my able-bodied seamanship papers. I am very proud to have them still in active condition.

In the fall of 1926, I entered Union Theological Seminary, and took my Bachelor of Divinity degree in 1929. In 1928 I was married. I served a term as a pastor in Amityville, Long Island, at the Methodist Church, and then transferred, as assistant pastor in charge of education and young people's work, to Central Methodist Church in Brooklyn. After a somewhat stormy career there, I was transferred to New Haven, Connecticut, where I had a church that was in the industrial section of that city, with a large proportion of the members of the parish out of work. It was in 1933 at the depth of the depression, and labor was just beginning to get into its historic struggles to organize.

I was engaged part time in activities as an organizer for the American Federation of Labor, but found my chief activity in the field of workers' education. This got me into the center of some of the disturbances that took place in New England, which was the scene of the Colt Firearms strike in 1934 and 1935, the Whitney-Blake struggle, and the Remington Rand affair where the famous Mohawk Valley formula was evolved.

I came into New York again in 1936 to direct the workers' education program of the WPA, and then went to work for the Resettlement Administration in the South, where I handled labor relations on a series of large construction projects. I remained with the labor division of the Resettlement Administration until, five years later, it became the Farm Security Administration, and then, with the coming of the war, I became the executive assistant of the Labor-Management Committee of the War Manpower Commission. The development of the labor-management cooperative efforts during the period of war production programs was most interesting and exciting.

When war work slacked off in the summer of 1944, I went to the American Federation of Labor to take up my present work of developing its social security program.

That is the brief framework of chronology on which the inner and more important experiences must be based. As I stated, I think that the greatest single influence which remains with me, and will probably remain with me all my life, was the combination of social zeal and religious fervor that expressed itself in the life and interests of my father. In a way, however, I got a miscue from my father. I thought his faith so reasonable that other people could be inspired to move along the same lines and with the same interest, if the same kind of reasonable faith were spread.

Another very profound influence running parallel to this was the fact that my work experience developed my firmest friendships among working people. My own little town was a very democratic community in most respects, but it had the division between the workers and others, though many of us were unconscious of it at that time. Yet my friends in high school and later in college were the sons of the working men in our town with whom I worked in the factories and on shipboard in the summer time. I tasted early the kind of fellowship that is much more real than one gets in a fraternity. It is much more real than one gets in a classroom in a university. I was privileged, I would say, to taste the real fellowship that one gets from working with other men at common tasks in industry, and sharing with them the problems with which they are confronted.

This experience was stimulated and to some extent rationalized when I began to study for the Christian ministry. I felt I should take something more practical than the usual courses, so I carried a double major in my undergraduate work: a major in English Bible, and a major in economics. I felt that my life work was an effort to weld these two together, and to try to achieve some goals of justice through a religious approach.

In Union Seminary, I carried a major in the philosophy of religion, but added many hours of study in the field of Christian ethics under the leadership of Harry Ward and Reinhold Niebuhr. A number of my teachers at the time asked me why I chose as a subject for my thesis, "The Emergence of Theism Among the

Greek Tragedians," for it was not consistent with my activities on and off the campus, but I had a very definite idea about it. I said, "Now, if I write my thesis under Harry Ward, I am going to get into all kinds of activities that are going to lead me far afield." I had written some term papers for Dr. Ward. If you were writing about labor problems, he was never satisfied unless you had got on the picket line, talked to the leader of the union, and included in your paper your interviews with union leaders and with management, where possible. I said, "If I write a thesis under that man, it is going to take forever to do it. So I am going to write a thesis that can be done on rainy days and nights in the library. Nothing new is likely to turn up. It will be on a topic so dead that the record is all completed." I deliberately took a subject which gave me plenty of time to follow what was listed as my minor course, but was actually my major in terms of interest.

Another great experience, which was shared by millions of people, was the depression of the early 1930's. At that time, I was the assistant pastor of a large downtown church in Brooklyn. That was an experience of some considerable disillusionment. I saw the contrast between great, rich city churches and the poor around them. For the first time I got a realistic look at ecclesiastical politics and machinery. I saw the contrast every day as I drove to work from our apartment to my study. In those days, I could never come to work in the city of Brooklyn without steering around people's household goods which were being set out on the sidewalk. Then I came to a beautifully appointed study with leaded-glass windows and all the accoutrements and symbols of prosperity. Physically, it was right at that great intersection in Brooklyn where the BMT and the IRT and the Long Island Railroad come together, and yet it seemed to me to be remote spiritually.

On summer nights when I was in my study, I could throw open the windows and hear men on soap boxes talking to the people down on the square beneath, across at the old loading platform. I would go down and stand on the edge of the group, and listen to them, and wonder why their hearers were interested. I felt that the church really had something more vital and relevant to the needs of these people; yet the soap box orators could bridge the gap, while we could not.

While I was still an assistant minister, I was called one night and told I had been selected to direct the relief work of the Brooklyn Federation of Churches. I did not have any choice about it. It was a call from my bishop. As the Protestant Church had no established relief organization, my job was to develop an organization that could handle relief among the five hundred and twenty-eight Protestant parishes in the Brooklyn Church and Mission Federation.

I worked pretty hard at that, but also did a great deal of educational work. I remember how the interviewers would bring back special problems to my office, where I would often hide because it was not easy to see those hordes of people. Day in and day out, month in and month out, I saw people cut loose from all their standards and all their past experiences, coming to a relief office for the first time. Yet I saw that they were completely without any understanding of the significance and meaning of the experiences through which they were passing.

That was my first experience with workers' education. I organized some of the teachers on relief into teaching classes. I got in touch with some of the unions that were carrying on workers' education. I said, "We have not only got to give them bread cards, but must also tell them what the experiences they are passing through mean to them, and to the society of which they are a part."

But this was not working through the Church. Finally, I decided to make one more effort to work through a church organization, and I asked the bishop to put me in an industrial area. He sent me to New Haven. When I made a survey, I found that fifty-five per cent of the heads of families in that parish were totally unemployed, and a little over half of those who had jobs were working no more than half time. The church was debt-ridden. It was loaded down with burdens almost impossible to carry.

Early in 1933, a friend of mine, who was then an organizer for the asbestos workers, asked me to go with him to a meeting in New Haven at which Secretary Perkins spoke. During the course of the meeting, Secretary Perkins said that under Section 7 (a) of the National Recovery Act, labor would have a new chance to organize. Then she called on the people who had any kind of labor experience to help with the problems of organization. My friend turned to me and said, "I guess that means you"; and I said in a moment of rashness, not knowing where it would lead, that I would be willing to help if I could. He told me there would be a meeting of the Central Trades Council that Thursday night. I went and found there a number of critical situations where I could be of some assistance in organizing with what little experience I had.

Soon after that, the Workers' Educational Bureau set up a program in connection with the Connecticut Federation of Labor. I found myself more and more led into its activities, so I asked in 1935 for a leave of absence from my church. That leave of absence has been extended up until the present time, and now I do not suppose it will ever come to an end.

During the course of this transition period, I was beginning to doubt the effectiveness of the kind of approach employed by the Church. I found that what I felt were the most dynamic elements of our religion, both in the New Testament and in the prophets of the Old Testament, had been ruined for many church members. They did not want to be told, for example, that Moses led the first great walkout, and that the name of the second book of our Bible, Exodus, was just a Latinized name for walkout. They did not want to be told that the prophets of Israel had themselves rebelled against formalism in religion in an effort to establish religion on an ethical basis. They felt that kind of interpretation more or less spoiled for them the most precious part of the religious heritage which they had learned at their mother's knee. I suppose it did, although perhaps the clumsiness of my presentation was partially responsible.

This would have led to blind frustration, had it not been for the outlet that was afforded by the labor unions. At Hartford, where two thousand workers at the Colt Patent Firearms Company had been out on the sidewalks for weeks trying to get recognition of their right to organize and bargain collectively, I got an entirely different reception when I told them that Moses had led the first walkout. They were experiencing the real economic, moral, and ethical problems of the time.

Actually, what I meant to be union talks came closer to religion than the things I was able to preach from my pulpit. I ruminated on that a good bit, and I began to wonder more and more about the relationship of religious life and religious experience to the problems that people had in their lives. I decided that preaching for the most part was pretty empty stuff.

The reason is this. Preaching, for at least one of its functions, should do something pretty much like the kind of a thing accomplished by the talk a football coach delivers to his team between halves. He has to pep up the players. He has to tell the boys with bruised shins and banged-up collar bones that they are out there giving themselves for old Alma Mater. The pep talk has meaning because he is talking between halves to the boys who are out in the thick of the game. But much of our preaching has no meaning because we are talking to people who are not engaged in the struggle. When we sing, "Faith of our fathers, living faith," it cannot be meaningful for people who have never been near a dungeon, who have never been burned or even singed with fire, and who have never been threatened with the sword. The thing that we are doing to a large extent, I feel rightly or wrongly, is giving a pep talk to boys who have never been near the scrimmage line.

That is the reason for much of the lack of reality in the Church's work. It lacked reality during the depression because the institution was not geared to meet the problems that were real and vital to the people of that time. Most of my people in the New Haven church worked in Winchester's plant. They lived in the shadow of the Winchester plant—a deep shadow that fell over the lives of all of them. Yet when they came to church on Sunday they did not want to hear about those problems. They wanted to dress up to look like the boss on Sunday. Their actions imitated the boss. One day a week they wanted to live the life of people whom they saw in these enviable, higher positions, under whose rule they lived. They did not want to break that illusion. They were trying to get away from the problems of workers one day a week. I am not sure but that there was a good bit of right on their side, but still they were escaping much of reality in their religious life.

All of this had a great deal to do with my inner feelings and adjustments. I am not attempting to overidealize the labor movement when I say that it supplied my spiritual needs at that time. In the struggles of the working people to equalize their power through collective action with the power of the overlords of industry, there emerged a spiritual quality that was very sincere and very real. It exists and will continue to exist.

Such were my reasons for moving from one channel of service to another. My own basic beliefs were not seriously altered in the transition. I have the same faith that was given me from my earliest years in the abiding quality of spiritual values. That faith is even deeper, despite all the disillusionment that the years have brought me. I have a confidence that this is a moral world which is the object of God's concern. Many of the philosophical problems that seemed to perplex those with whom I was in the seminary do not bother me much, probably because I do not have time really to think about them. I am not sure that this is good. Perhaps my own philosophy should have a more reasonable basis, but as it is I accept a good deal about the worthwhileness of the values I am trying to achieve without analyzing them.

As to institutionalized religion, there is a conflict there that I am not sure can be resolved. I never had a quarrel or broke with the Church. I am not saying nor have I said to men in the ministry that they should get out of the Church. I do not believe that at all. I am less inclined to believe it now than I ever was. It was the thing for me to do, but that does not mean at all that it is the thing for any other person to do.

There are many fronts on which the fight for the betterment of men must take place: the educational front, the religious field of service, and the field directly connected with organized labor. Perhaps the latter can be compared with the front line, where the bayonet work against the forces of greed is taking place; but the other branches of service, just as in an army, need to carry on. No invidious comparison should be made between them. There is a great service to be performed toward ethical and social ends by organized religion and we who are in the organized labor movement would like the support and assistance that are given by liberal religious institutions to increase tremendously.

But strangely enough, to complete this highly subjective account, for some reason I do not personally rely on institutionalized religious services. Perhaps this is simply because, being away a great deal and working, as my wife says, a twelve-hour day getting a seven-hour day for other people, home hours are too precious; or perhaps it is because I found, on a somewhat limited survey, that Washington churches have not satisfied me. In any case, I never go to church.

The small churches where men have zeal and fire are so small that they are not satisfying, and where the churches are large enough to have a good pipe organ, it seems that the ministers are all steeped in the conservative point of view. However, maybe it is I, and not the organ, that is out of tune. In any event, I find that my own inspiration, rightly or wrongly, comes more from an enjoyment of music, keeping alive an interest in great literature, and from such other resources as I can draw on myself. After the few times I have been to church in Washington, it has taken me about six weeks to get my real interest back. In all fairness I should mention that the shortcomings of this particular phase of my religious life may be attested by the fact that it has been found completely unsatisfying to my seventeen year old daughter. She is a very faithful attendant at Sunday school and church. She joined a Quaker community of her own volition and was not satisfied until she entered a Quaker school where she is a leader in the religious activities of the campus.

I have found in the very conflicts into which my chosen way of life has led me, a peace that I have not known anywhere else.

Maybe it is a curious twist of nature, but only when engaged in a good hard fight to accomplish something to improve life for the workers in our unions, do I find an inner peace and satisfaction that I think is comparable to religious experience.

XVII

I WENT BACK TO CHURCH

BY

ELLIS F. VAN RIPER

Organizer, Transport Workers Union

I have been in the labor movement since I was fourteen years old, when my father died, and that is twenty-one years ago. I come from a background of a family that has been in the trade union movement ever since bona fide trade unions existed in New York. I am the family's black sheep because all of my family are in the A. F. of L., and I am the only one in the CIO.

I was born and brought up in the church, but I left it when I was sixteen. My parents were both religious, especially my mother, and my father was a deacon in the Baptist Church. It was a "hardshell" church. You could not do a lot of things because they were not right, and we youngsters felt there were not a lot of things you could do because they were right. The result was that, when I was sixteen, I left the church to stay away for approximately six or seven years.

While I was in the church, I belonged to a lot of those organizations on the fringe of the social order. There are a great many of them in the church. They really do not do anything about changing the social order; they only flit around the outside a bit. I had my share of all of them and did not feel that they had anything for me, for going on inside of me at that time was a conflict.

I had come from a trade union background. I was active in the various local strikes and the labor activity that was going on in the building trades in New York City, but I felt the definite gap between my spiritual life and everyday living. At various times I was as pious as could be in a holy roller sort of way, and almost the next moment I would be radically extreme, and all sorts of spiritual values would go by the board.

Then in 1930 I started two and a half years of unemployment. The building trades went to pot. There were no jobs. I had trained for seven years in school and on the job for my work, and now I could not find work. All kinds of thoughts went through my head. I saw the values on which I had based my life up to that time crashing around me. The material basis for my life was not there any more.

I had various kinds of hates, fears, and resentments, and a decided class feeling began to grow in me during that period. I learned to hate, not only people who I felt were responsible for the depression, but certain people in the labor movement who through pull and protection were keeping me from the kind of employment I thought I could get.

Whether it was true or not is another question. The thought was there. There was a gnawing fear at the bottom of my heart all the time. I had a mother to support. I was not so worried about myself, but it was a question of feeding her, taking care of the home, the bills, and all that went with it. That fear never left me even when I went to sleep at night.

But all through this particular situation, there was one thing that stood out, and that was my mother's particular personal faith. There were times in my house when there was not a nickel for the next day's food. All through that particular period, my mother never had any doubt in her mind but that there would be food on the table next day, and money for it. In two and one half years, I never saw her disappointed. That had its direct effect upon me personally. I realized there was something she had that I did not have, and I went back to church to find it after seven years away.

She had a curious statement which I have never forgotten: "When God closes one door, He always opens one in another room, and it always takes you a few minutes to walk across the room."

I went back to church, and they welcomed me with open arms. Within three months I, who had not been to church in seven years, was the assistant superintendent of the Sunday school. They gave me a class of boys twelve years old. Those of you who do any Sunday school work know what the twelve year old boys are. May the Lord have mercy on me and them for what they learned in the first classes, because the battle that had been going on before I left the church was still going on inside me. I still had not been able to reconcile the two areas of my life. I needed something, for I had not been able to bridge the gap between the two. It was not until 1934 that I met a minister in my own church who seemed to sense almost immediately the conflict that was going on inside of me. He got hold of me, and I spent some long and torturous hours with him in his study. He helped me to find, for the first time, a personal faith. He helped me with some very definite personal problems that I had: moral problems, problems in relationships with people, my general attitude, and my beliefs. And he stayed with me. It was not a Sunday morning half-hour thing. Sometimes it was four and five days a week for weeks on end.

He did this for me, and I have always been grateful. One thing he told me was not to accept the dogma of the labor movement, or the dogma of the church, as fact, without having thought it through for myself first of all in the light of the experience which I was gaining personally. That I tried to do. In the process of trying to think through these matters and apply them to the community and the social activities in which I was engaged at that time, a personal faith was coming to me. The conflict that was in me began to go away. I cannot tell you when it stopped, or when it began, or when I could say it had gone. There are times now when I am not so sure of things, but definitely the uneasiness that I had about the correlation of the two areas of my life went away, and I found that I was beginning to find a vision for myself of my place, my spot, my particular place, in the scheme of things as an individual, not as a big shot, but just as plain John Doe in the community.

I began to see what labor was talking about in its long-range planning and vision. I had held a union card up to that time, perhaps for ten or eleven years, but now I began to lift my nose up off the individual grindstone and look ahead to see what the labor movement was trying to do. As a result, I became of more value to the labor movement. Up to that time, I had been nothing more than just another one of the boys that picked up a sign when he was told to pick it up, went to meetings when the meetings were called, raised his hand and voted on the various issues, and so on; but now I began to see that something more was required of me than just paying my dues and attending meetings.

The result was that, with increased vision and articulateness, came increased responsibility. It is a funny thing, but in the labor movement, when you open your mouth, you get a job; the more you open it, the more work you get. The fellow that is foolish enough to say what he thinks and shows he has at least a little mind, right away gets a job to do. I did that and responsibility came along with it. First I was shop steward, then shop chairman, then chairman of the grievance committee in a plant where there were twenty-five hundred men. Later I was on the executive board and, finally, organizer for the union. Those steps came over a period of five or six years.

I have said enough to indicate my background, so now I would like to describe what I think are the basic things on which I am moving, my basic convictions.

First of all, let me say I am not a Communist; I am not a So-cialist; I am not a capitalist; I am not a Fascist. I am just a plain, ordinary Christian, and that is a lot more revolutionary than the other four. I feel that any society that deserves the name of Chris-tian, or claims to have moral or spiritual foundations, must include five basic rights for every person born into that society. To be sure, a Christian has no rights; he has only responsibilities. Therefore these five rights are not my rights; they are my neighbor's rights and my responsibility: adequate food, clothing, shelter, education, and health. Above and beyond them you can have all the free enterprise and individual competition you want, but you must pro-vide them if you want to earn the name of Christian for your society.

The labor movement is a major vehicle for bringing these things to the community. The place of the church is in supplying the dynamic force to those in the community who are doing the job. Up to the present time, much of what passes for church and labor activity is what I like to call "tail-end activity." There are certain groups in the church and labor field who are trying to make the labor movement the tail end of the church, and the church the tail end of the labor movement. Both are wrong as I see it.

The church and labor should be on a cooperative basis, not a competitive basis. Neither should control nor dominate the other; neither should interfere with the inner workings of the other. We do not expect and do not want the church to take over the education of the worker. We have plenty of trained men to do that job. However, we do need from the church men who have personal character, personal faith, the power to get along with people, and power to see and envision moral and social implications in the community.

It must also be said, however, that there are definite places where we must cooperate with groups who are not necessarily Christian or spiritually minded. There are certain objectives and certain Christian activities which we share with non-Christians. I will break with them only at one point, and that is at the point where I am forced to compromise my personal moral and spiritual convictions; but in doing that, I am not going to get all mixed up in witch hunting, and be anti-this, or anti-that, or anti-something-else. There is a definite field of correlation of the church and labor, and there are also some places where we must break with our more extreme beliefs both in the church and in the labor movement.

The difference, as I see it, between Christian, spiritually minded people in the community and those who are working only for a better social order, is at one basic point. It is this: there are people trying to create a better world who have the welfare of the people only in their head; we Christians, instead of having that in our head alone, must have it in our hearts as well. If our interest in others is based on moral and spiritual foundations, the foundations must be in the heart, as well as in the head.

But to have it in the heart without something in the head is no good either. There is a verse in Second Timothy, the first chapter, which says that God has not given us a spirit of cowardice, but a spirit of love, power, and sound judgment. Too many of us who are interested in church and labor stop at the first two and forget the sound judgment. We are long on love, a pious kind of thing, and long on power, but very short when it comes to sound judgment. If you are going to get somebody to fix a faucet, you do not get a carpenter, you get a plumber; and if you want a carpentry job done, you get a carpenter because he is a carpenter, not because he is a Christian carpenter. That illustrates the place where we need to improve our thinking.

I do not expect to see the church crusade for any particular social or political action. There is room in the church for differences, political, social, and economic; but there is no room for class conflict. On the other hand, I think we should get faith out of the pews into the streets where the people can find it.

We must begin to change some of the moral thinking of the church. True, adultery, murder, and thieving are sin, but what about social dislocation? What about the exploitation of individuals and groups? We must begin to put that kind of social sin in the same classification as personal sin, and act against it with the same vigor and drive that we put into, for instance, getting rid of corner beer gardens or gambling. These last are the problems with which the church ordinarily busies itself. Meanwhile the world is going to hell. Two blocks away people are out on picket lines. There is a dislocation of our economy based on personal individual selfishness. We are busy worrying about budgets and about the next conference when there are people on the corner with picket signs over their shoulders.

I personally have come to find just as much moral and spiritual satisfaction in the work I am doing in the labor movement as I do in communion on a Sunday morning. I cannot see any difference. I get the same sense of peace and satisfaction. I do not mean peace in the outward sense, because there is not much peace in the labor movement at the present time, but the inner sense of well being, the inner sense that you are in the right spot and doing the

right job according to your lights, the sense that you are doing
what God wants you to do at the moment.

In the church, we pass resolutions and issue pamphlets, but the
average parishioner is at least ten years behind the national leaders
of his church in these matters. The top leaders of the church and
the top leaders of labor get together easily. You telephone and get
them together. They sit down around a table, discuss, and find out
that they agree; but the closer you get to the parish church and
synagogue, the more hostile is the relationship, until when you
finally get to the parish pew it is almost open warfare. That is
where the job needs to be done, where I am hoping to do the job,
where I am trying to direct my activities.

The Federal Council of Churches is fine, and various other
groups and social commissions are all fine and all good, but it is
on the parish level where the relationship breaks down. The average
parish minister does not even know in some cases what the thinking of his church is on the social issues, and when he is brought face
to face with it, he is the most surprised man in the world and
wonders how he ever got into such a Communistic organization.

These things are a very serious problem because we have people
in the labor movement who are there, not because they are going
to get a few dollars, but because they feel they are doing something to build a better America. If leadership in the labor movement goes to the radical extreme, then churchmen will have to share
the blame for letting the extremists take it by forfeit. There is nothing inherent in the labor movement that would make this happen,
for the basic ideals of the labor movement are the basic ideals of the
church. We do not go around saving souls in the labor movement,
but we are saving the people economically and politically.

Without moral and spiritual values in the battle for a better
world, the social vision quickly deteriorates into class warfare. In
the case of half the people, somebody spat on their shoes and they
have been mad ever since, and so they are trying to change the
world from hate, not from love.

We have to have the kind of consciousness which makes your
foot cold when there is a hole in my shoe. You do not develop

that feeling with textbooks. You do not do it by passing resolutions. You cannot love people by telephone. You have to love them by getting to know them.

I personally do not want to see any minister or rabbi on the picket line unless he believes with all his heart and soul that this is right. I do not want to see him on the picket line because it is the smart thing to do—then he is a liability and not an asset. I want to see him there because his parishioners are on that line. I want to see him there because Henry Smith, John Jones, and Frank Whatever-his-name-is, who belong to his congregation, are in trouble. They are in a situation where emotions run wild. Reason does not always rule, and so they need someone to give them a sense of direction and the knowledge that somebody does care. Long after the newspaper pictures have disappeared and people no longer read the newspaper clippings, the men in the unions will talk about Pastor Smith or Rabbi Cohen who assisted them during their trouble. An act of that sort will be almost legendary if it is done in the right spirit. The men themselves will respond.

I agree wholeheartedly with Kermit Eby who said that we in the church and in the synagogue belong by the side of the labor movement as long as it is the agent of the people. We must break with it only when it becomes an agent of power. That is my position. As a Christian, I will work side by side with all kinds of people in the labor movement, whoever they may be. I will break with them only when they become agents of power. Let me say that this happens only very rarely and then only in individual cases. I have the utmost confidence in the more intelligent top leadership of our labor movement. It is far more able than I to see the problems ahead. I know that within it are many men who are morally and spiritually motivated. If we were to take a cross section of the leadership of the labor movement, we would be amazed to find how many of them got their earliest training in the church and synagogue, and amazed at the basic principles on which they make their decisions.

INDEX

Index *179*

planning by, 16-18; racial segregation in, 69; training schools of, 80
franchise. *See* vote
free enterprise, 16, 47
French influence, 79
Fritchie, Barbara, 39
full employment, 17, 46-47, 94, 96, 98, 114-115
Functions of the Executive, The (Barnard), 5n

Gallup Poll, 55
Germans, as a minority group, 84
God, belief in, 127, 130-133, 146-147, 154
Gompers, Samuel, 24, 39, 49, 50, 51, 53, 56
Goodrich, Carter, paper by, 87-90
government. *See* federal government
governments, in International Labor Organization, 87-90
Grant, Madison, 64
Green, Dwight H., 72
Green, William, 25
groups: for human satisfaction, 3-10, 124; intolerance in, 7; minority, 61-76, 77-86, 95-98, 109-111, 115, 147-148, 150, 152-153; mixture of, 136

Hamilton Report on Manufactures, 16
Hartford, Conn., 163-164
Harvard Union Fellowships, 42
Harvard University, representative from, 1
Haywood, Bill, 50
health protection, 18, 21, 25
Hearst, William Randolph, 127-129
Herald-Examiner, 128-129
Hillman, Sidney, 54, 59
History of Labor in the United States, 33
Hocking, William Ernest, 146
Hoffmann, Alfred, paper by, 135-144
hosiery union, 137-144
housing, racial segregation in, 66
human relations, 173-176; labor relations as, 135-144; and the worker, 2-10

imperialism, 15
India, as a minority, 61

industry: human problems of, 2-10, 139-140; influence of, 12, 34, 40-41, 108-109; racial discrimination in, 67-68, 78-86; and worker education, 102. *See also* employers
Industry Committees, 90
international cartels, 16
International Labor Organization, 87-90
International Ladies' Garment Workers' Union, representative from, 33
international security, and labor, 151
intolerance, in groups, 7. *See also* discrimination
Irish, as a minority group, 84

Jamaica, 62
Jews, discrimination against, 65, 75. *See also* Judaism
Jim Crow system, 63-64
jobs, meaningful, 1-10. *See also* employment
Jones, John Paul, 150
Jones, Mother, 39
Judaism, 118; and organized labor, 109-110, 116. *See also* Jews

Kelley, Florence, 148
Kelly, Edward J., 72
Know-Nothing Party, 84
Koestler, Arthur, 125
Ku Klux Klan, 84, 96

labor: and the Church, 91-116; the jobs of, 1-10; and minority groups, 61-76, 77-86, 109-110, 115. *See also* labor, organized
labor, organized: and challenge to religion, 91-98; and children, 19-31; and the Church, 91-116; and the community, 1-90, 140-143, 152, 171-176; and education, 11, 12, 18, 20, 21-22, 24, 25-26, 30, 33-48, 102, 121, 137, 162-163; international, 87-90; leaders of, 99-103, 117-176; and the national welfare, 11-18, 151; and the Negro, 67-68, 69-70, 71, 79, 83-85, 95, 109-111, 115; and politics, 49-60, 152; reconciliation with